THE BEST BOOK
OF USELESS
INFORMATION
EVER

THE BEST BOOK OF USELESS INFORMATION EVER

BY NOEL BOTHAM

JOHN BLAKE

Published by John Blake Publishing Ltd,
3, Bramber Court, 2 Bramber Road,
London W14 9PB, England

www.blake.co.uk

First published in Hardback in 2005

ISBN 1 84454 175 4

British Library Cataloguing-in-Publication Data:

A catalogue record for this book is available from the British Library.

Design by www.envydesign.co.uk

Printed in Great Britain by Creative Print and Design

1 3 5 7 9 10 8 6 4 2

© Text copyright Noel Botham 2005

Papers used by John Blake Publishing are natural, recyclable products made from
wood grown in sustainable forests. The manufacturing processes conform to the
environmental regulations of the country of origin.

Every attempt has been made to contact the relevant copyright-holders, but some
were unobtainable. We would be grateful if the appropriate people could contact us.

CONTENTS

PEOPLE AND PLACES

———————— PEOPLE AND PLACES ————————

- The state of Alaska has the most people per population that walk to work in the whole of the United States.

- The busiest stretch of highway in the US is New York's George Washington Bridge.

- Ropesville, Lariat and Loop are all towns in Texas.

- Venetian blinds were invented in Japan.

- In Venice, Venetian blinds are known as 'Persian blinds'.

- If you head directly south from Detroit, the first foreign country you will enter is Canada.

- One in every three people in Israel uses a mobile phone.

- Sixty per cent of the country of Liechtenstein's GDP is generated from the sale of false teeth.

- In the US, 166,875,000,000 pieces of mail are delivered each year.

- Oklahoma is the US state with the highest population of Native Americans. It has no Indian Reservations.

——————— PEOPLE AND PLACES ———————

- The Statue of Liberty's fingernails weigh about 100lb apiece.

- In Kenya, they don't drive on the right or left side of the street in particular, just on whichever side is smoother.

- The state of Maryland has no natural lakes.

- JELL-O [jelly] was declared the 'official state snack' of Utah in January 2001.

- Scandinavian folklore records that trolls only come out at night because sunlight would turn them to stone.

- 1,525,000,000 miles of telephone wire are strung across the Unites States.

- Wyoming Valley is so difficult to find because it is in Pennsylvania.

- After Canada and Mexico, Russia is the nearest neighbour to the United States. Siberia's easternmost point is just 56 miles from Alaska. In fact, in the middle of the Bering Strait, Russia's Big Diomede Island and the US's Little Diomede Island are only two miles apart.

PEOPLE AND PLACES

- The parents of the groom pay for the weddings in Thailand.

- One US state no longer exists. In 1784, the US had a state called Franklin, named after Benjamin Franklin. But four years later, it was incorporated into Tennessee.

- In Tibet, there is actually a practice called 'polyandry' where many men, usually brothers, marry a single woman.

- The coastline around Lake Sakawea in North Dakota is longer than the California coastline along the Pacific Ocean

- Brooklyn is the Dutch name for 'broken valley'.

- Danishes are called Vienna cakes in Denmark, and Spanish rice is unknown in Spain.

- Birkenhead Park was the inspiration for New York's Central Park as it was the world's first urban park.

- The city of Nottingham was the first city to have Braille signs in the UK.

- Minnesota has 99 lakes named Mud Lake.

PEOPLE AND PLACES

- At the turn of the century, the New Brighton Tower (located atop the tower ballroom) was higher than the Blackpool Tower. The steel tower was taken down between 1919 and 1921.

- Fort Worth Texas was never a fort.

- Legend has it that, when Burmese women are making beer, they need to avoid having sex or the beer will be bitter.

- Kitsap County, Washington, was originally called Slaughter County, and the first hotel there was called the Slaughter House.

- Saunas outnumber cars in Finland.

- Although Argentina's name means 'Land of Silver', there is actually very little silver there. It was misnamed by explorers who thought they saw veins of the metal there.

- The state of California raises the most turkeys in the US.

- America's first stock exchange was the Philadelphia Stock Exchange, established in 1791.

--- **PEOPLE AND PLACES** ---

- Bagpipes, although identified with Scotland, are actually a very ancient instrument, introduced into the British Isles by the Romans.

- Antarctica is visited by over 10,000 tourists a year.

- The Pony Express, one of the most famous chapters in US history, only lasted one year, from 1860 to 1861.

- There are four states where the first letter of the capital city is the same letter as the first letter of the state: Dover, Delaware; Honolulu, Hawaii; Indianapolis, Indiana; and Oklahoma City, Oklahoma.

- Andorra, a tiny country on the border between France and Spain, has the longest average lifespan: 83.49 years.

- Oregon has the most ghost towns of any state.

- Construction of the Notre Dame Cathedral in Strasbourg started in 1015, but it was not until 1439 that the spire was completed.

- There are more Rolls-Royces in Hong Kong than anywhere else in the world.

———————— **PEOPLE AND PLACES** ————————

- Japan has 130 times more people per square mile than the state of Montana.

- The most expensive commercial real estate in the world is in Tokyo. The second most expensive is 57th Street in New York City.

- Mt. Everest grows about 4mm a year: the two tectonic plates of Asia and India, which collided millions of years ago to form the Himalayas, continue to press against each other, causing the Himalayan peaks to grow slightly each year.

- The Norman Baron Eudo Dapifer built Colchester Castle, 1075–1080, around the podium of the Roman temple of Claudius, creating the largest Norman keep in Britain.

- Japanese rickshaws were invented by an American, Reverend Jonathan Scobie, who visited Okinawa in 1869.

- In Tokyo, to buy a three-line classified ad in the newspaper costs £1,800 per day.

- Antarctica has only one ATM machine.

PEOPLE AND PLACES

- Hawaiian lore teaches that the earth mother Papa mated with the sky father Wakea to give birth to the Hawaiian Islands.

- There are many kremlins in the Soviet Union. Kremlin just means the centre of government, which can be applied to the government buildings in any town.

- The per capita use of soap in Great Britain is 40 ounces per year. In France, it is only 22.6 ounces per year.

- There is a monastery in Ethiopia that can be entered only by climbing up a rope dropped over the edge of a cliff.

- In Turkey, when someone is in mourning, they wear purple clothing, not black.

- The desert country of Saudi Arabia must import sand from other countries. This is because their desert sand is not suitable for building construction.

- In Tibet, some women have special metal instruments used for picking their noses.

- There is a chemical waste dump in the Soviet Union that is twice as big as the whole state of Vermont.

PEOPLE AND PLACES

● Nights in the tropics are warm because moist air retains heat well. Desert nights get cold rapidly because dry air does not hold heat to the same degree.

● Deep in the jungles of South America, a tribe of primitive people was discovered. Everyone had forgotten how to make fire and therefore they carefully guarded piles of burning embers. If all their fires went out, they would have been doomed to existence without fire.

● The largest Gothic cathedral is not in Rome or Paris, but on Amsterdam Avenue in New York City.

● The smallest church in the world is in Kentucky. There is room inside for three people.

● Only 8.5% of all Alaskans are Eskimos.

● Reno, Nevada, is further west than Los Angeles, California.

● Twenty-four per cent of Los Angeles, California, is road and parking lots for cars.

● There is a house in Margate, New Jersey, that is made in the shape of an elephant. A home in Norman, Oklahoma is shaped like a chicken.

─────────── **PEOPLE AND PLACES** ───────────

- There is a house in Massachusetts which is made entirely ✓
from newspapers. The floors, walls and even the furniture
is made from newspaper.

- Another house, this one in Canada, is made of 18,000
discarded glass bottles.

- The Greek word for brotherly love is Philadelphia.

- The worst American city to live in, from the viewpoint
of air pollution, is St Louis, Missouri.

- Over half of all Americans travel more than a million
miles in their lifetimes.

- American drivers average about 8,200 miles a year.

THINGS
CELEBRITIES
SAY

—————— THINGS CELEBRITIES SAY ——————

● 'I can't really remember the names of the clubs that we went to.'

> SHAQUILLE O'NEAL, BASKETBALL PLAYER,
> ON WHETHER HE HAD VISITED THE PARTHENON
> DURING HIS VISIT TO GREECE

● 'It's nice, it gives you a feeling of security so that if something breaks we know we can always call a guy over and he'll bring a drill or something.'

> BROOKE SHIELDS, ON WHY IT WAS GOOD TO LIVE IN A
> CO-ED DORMITORY WHEN SHE WAS IN COLLEGE

● 'You don't have to be the Dalai Lama to tell people that life's about change.'

> JOHN CLEESE

● 'Hearthrob are a dime a dozen.'

> BRAD PITT

● 'My weaknesses have always been food and men – in that order.'

> DOLLY PARTON

● 'I just want to conquer people and their souls.'

> MIKE TYSON

———————— **THINGS CELEBRITIES SAY** ————————

● 'After doing *One Fine Day* and playing a pediatrician on *ER*, I'll never have kids. I'm going to have a vasectomy.'

GEORGE CLOONEY

● 'Alex Ferguson is the best manager I've ever had at this level. Well, he's the only manager I've actually had at this level. But he's the best manager I've ever had.'

DAVID BECKHAM

● 'Once you've been really "bad"' in a movie, there's a certain kind of fearlessness you develop.'

JACK NICHOLSON

● 'I carried my Oscar to bed with me. My first and only three-way happened that night.'

HALLE BERRY

● 'No one is more enslaved than a slave who doesn't think they're enslaved.'

KATE BECKINSALE

● 'I'd like to put on buckskins and a ponytail and go underwater with a reed, hiding from the Indians… To me, that's sexy!'

KEVIN COSTNER

——————— **THINGS CELEBRITIES SAY** ———————

● 'Hugh Grant and I both laugh and cringe at the same things, worship the same books, eat the same food, hate central heating and sleep with the window open. I thought these things were vital, but being two peas in a pod ended up not being enough.'

ELIZABETH HURLEY

● 'I don't have a boyfriend right now. I'm looking for anyone with a job that I don't have to support.'

ANNA NICOLE SMITH

● 'I've never had a problem with drugs. I've had problems with the police.'

KEITH RICHARDS

● 'Men cheat for the same reason that dogs lick their balls… because they can.'

KIM CATTRALL

● 'I always had a repulsive need to be something more than human.'

DAVID BOWIE

● 'You don't realise how useful a therapist is until you see one yourself and discover you have more problems than you ever dreamed of.'

CLAIRE DANES

———— THINGS CELEBRITIES SAY ————

- 'Through years of experience I have found that air offers less resistance than dirt.'

  JACK NICKLAUS

- 'You mean they've scheduled Yom Kippur opposite *Charlie's Angels*?'

  FRED SILVERMAN, TV PROGRAMMER, WHEN TOLD THAT
  YOM KIPPUR WOULD FALL ON A WEDNESDAY

- 'I don't think I'm too thin at all. I understand when people say, "Well, your face gets gaunt," but, to get your bottom half to be the right size, your face might have to be a little gaunt. You choose your battles.'

  COURTNEY COX

- 'Well the joke is, of course, there is no British Empire left, is there? So I'm dame of a great big zero.'

  HELEN MIRREN, ON RECEIVING A ROYAL HONOUR

- 'My biggest nightmare is I'm driving home and get sick and go to hospital. I say, "Please help me." And the people say, "Hey, you look like …" And I'm dying while they're wondering whether I'm Barbra Streisand.'

  BARBRA STREISAND

——— THINGS CELEBRITIES SAY———

- 'What's the point of doing something good if nobody's watching?'

  NICOLE KIDMAN

- 'I'm in trouble because I'm normal and slightly arrogant. A lot of people don't like themselves and I happen to be totally in love with myself.'

  MIKE TYSON

- 'I do have big tits. Always had 'em – pushed 'em up, whacked 'em around. Why not make fun of 'em? I've made a fortune with 'em.'

  DOLLY PARTON

- 'I owe a lot to my parents, especially my mother and father.'

  GREG NORMAN

- 'I have to be careful to get out before I become the grotesque caricature of a hatchet-faced woman with big knockers.'

  JAMIE LEE CURTIS

- 'The biggest misconception people have about me is that I'm stupid.'

  BILLY IDOL

———— THINGS CELEBRITIES SAY ————

- 'When I was in prison, I was wrapped up in all those deep books. That Tolstoy crap – people shouldn't read that stuff.'

  MIKE TYSON

- 'Just let the wardrobe do the acting.'

  JACK NICHOLSON

- 'Big girls need big diamonds.'

  ELIZABETH TAYLOR

- 'Nothing irritates me more than chronic laziness in others. Mind you, it's only mental sloth I object to. Physical sloth can be heavenly.'

  ELIZABETH HURLEY

- 'I think in 20 years I'll be looked at like Bob Hope. Doing those president jokes and golf shit. It scares me.'

  EDDIE MURPHY

- 'If you talk bad about country music, it's like saying bad things about my momma. Them's fightin' words.'

  DOLLY PARTON

- 'Real freedom is having nothing. I was freer when I didn't have a cent.'

  MIKE TYSON

———— THINGS CELEBRITIES SAY ————

- 'From an early age I was aware of what America meant, and how the Marines at Camp Pendleton were ready to defend us at a moment's notice. I also remember what fabulous bodies those troops had.'

    HEATHER LOCKLEAR

- 'Now I can wear heels.'

    NICOLE KIDMAN, ON DIVORCING TOM CRUISE

- 'I could serve coffee using my rear as a ledge.'

    JENNIFER LOPEZ

- 'I just don't like the idea of her singing my songs. Who the hell does she thinks she is? The world doesn't need another Streisand!'

    BARBRA STREISAND, ON DIANA ROSS

- 'I never thought I was wasted, but I probably was.'

    KEITH RICHARDS

- 'Golf is a better game played downhill.'

    JACK NICKLAUS

- 'I will wear whatever and blow whomever I want as long as I can breathe and kneel.'

    KIM CATTRALL

———— THINGS CELEBRITIES SAY ————

- 'There are so many people out there taking the p*ss out of me that if I can't take the p*ss out of myself there's something going wrong.'

  VICTORIA BECKHAM

- 'There are two types of actors: those who say they want to be famous and those who are liars.'

  KEVIN BACON

- 'I'm only two years older than Brad Pitt, but I look a lot older, which used to greatly frustrate me. It doesn't any more. I don't have to fit into that category and get trounced by Tom Cruise and Brad.'

  GEORGE CLOONEY

- 'If I can get you to laugh with me, you like me better, which makes you more open to my ideas. And, if I can persuade you to laugh at the particular point I make, by laughing at it you acknowledge its truth.'

  JOHN CLEESE

- 'I used to do drugs, but don't tell anyone or it will ruin my image.'

  COURTNEY LOVE

———— **THINGS CELEBRITIES SAY** ————

● 'I think that everyone should get married at least once, so you can see what a silly, outdated institution it is.'

MADONNA

● 'I never diet. I smoke. I drink now and then. I never work out. I work very hard, and I am worth every cent.'

NAOMI CAMPBELL

● 'I have a love interest in every one of my films – a gun.'

ARNOLD SCHWARZENEGGER

● 'Just standing around looking beautiful is so boring.'

MICHELLE PFEIFFER

● 'I know there are nights when I have power, when I could put on something and walk in somewhere, and if there is a man who doesn't look at me, it's because he's gay.'

KATHLEEN TURNER

● 'If you're going to kick authority in the teeth, you might as well use two feet.'

KEITH RICHARDS

● 'I paid a worker at New York's zoo to reopen it just for me and Robin [Tyson's ex-wife]. When we got to the gorilla cage, there was one big silverback gorilla there

————— THINGS CELEBRITIES SAY —————

just bullying all the other gorillas. They were so powerful but their eyes were like an innocent infant. I offered the attendant $10,000 to open the cage and let me smash that silverback's snotbox! He declined.'

MIKE TYSON

• 'It's been seven years since I've had sex.'

ANNA NICOLE SMITH

• 'There's no drugs, no Tom in a dress, no psychiatrists.'

NICOLE KIDMAN

• 'Women don't want to hear what you think. Women want to hear what they think – in a deeper voice.'

BILL COSBY

• 'I don't want to ever, ever do something in life that isn't fun. Ever.'

JENNIFER LOVE HEWITT

• 'I found my inner bitch and ran with her.'

COURTNEY LOVE

• 'I don't want people to know what I'm actually like. It's not good for an actor.'

JACK NICHOLSON

—————— **THINGS CELEBRITIES SAY** ——————

- 'I have got little feet because nothing grows in
  the shade.'

  DOLLY PARTON

- 'Mr Right's coming, but he's in Africa, and he's walking.'

  OPRAH WINFREY

- 'I don't always wear underwear. When I'm in the heat,
  especially, I can't wear it. Like, if I'm wearing a flower
  dress, why do I have to wear underwear?'

  NAOMI CAMPBELL

- 'I hated singing. I wanted to be an actress. But I don't
  think I'd have made it any other way.'

  BARBRA STREISAND

- 'I'm afraid to be alone, I'm afraid not to be alone.
  I'm afraid of what I am, what I'm not, what I might
  become, what I might never become. I don't want to
  stay at my job for the rest of my life, but I'm afraid to
  leave. And I'm just tired, you know? I'm just so tired
  of being afraid.'

  MICHELLE PFEIFFER

- 'Children always understand. They have open minds.
  They have built-in shit detectors.'

  MADONNA

————— THINGS CELEBRITIES SAY —————

- 'How people keep correcting us when we are young! There is always some bad habit or other they tell us we ought to get over. Yet most bad habits are tools to help us through life.'

  JACK NICKLAUS

- 'I definitely want Brooklyn to be christened, but I don't know into what religion yet.'

  DAVID BECKHAM

- 'I always listen to *NSYNC's "Tearin' Up My Heart". It reminds me to wear a bra.'

  BRITNEY SPEARS

- 'He who laughs most learns best.'

  JOHN CLEESE

- 'Everyone probably thinks that I'm a raving nymphomaniac, that I have an insatiable sexual appetite, when the truth is I'd rather read a book.'

  MADONNA

- 'I'm not a woman, I'm a force of nature.'

  COURTNEY LOVE

———————— **THINGS CELEBRITIES SAY** ————————

● 'A word to the wise ain't necessary, it's the stupid ones who need the advice.'

BILL COSBY

● 'I feel safe in white because, deep down inside, I'm an angel.'

SEAN 'P DIDDY' COMBS

● 'I'm staggered by the question of what it's like to be a multimillionaire. I always have to remind myself that I am.'

BRUCE WILLIS

● 'I hope there's a tinge of disgrace about me. Hopefully, there's one good scandal left in me yet.'

DIANA RIGG

● 'I'd like to design something like a city or a museum. I want to do something hands on rather than just play golf which is the sport of the religious right.'

Brad Pitt

● 'If it's illegal to rock and roll, throw my ass in jail!'

Kurt Cobain

● 'So you know what I'm gonna do? I'm gonna do something really outrageous, I'm gonna tell the truth.'

John Travolta

———— **THINGS CELEBRITIES SAY** ————

● 'My mother never saw the irony in calling me a son-of-a-bitch.'

JACK NICHOLSON

● 'Any idiot can get laid when they're famous. That's easy. It's getting laid when you're not famous that takes some talent.'

KEVIN BACON

● 'I feel old when I see mousse in my opponent's hair.'

ANDRE AGASSI

● 'I don't think President Bush is doing anything at all about AIDS. In fact, I'm not sure he even knows how to spell AIDS.'

ELIZABETH TAYLOR

● 'Lots of people want to ride with you in the limo, but what you want is someone who will take the bus with you when the limo breaks down.'

OPRAH WINFREY

● 'I'm tough, ambitious, and I know exactly what I want. If that makes me a bitch, OK.'

MADONNA

———— THINGS CELEBRITIES SAY ————

• 'We are not that flash, me or the missus [Madonna].
  In fact, we are quite low-maintenance.'

  GUY RITCHIE

• 'I had a huge crush on Olga Korbut, the gymnast. The
  only other person was Cliff Richard, which is
  embarrassing – it means that when I was seven I had bad
  taste and was presumably gay.'

  HUGH GRANT

• 'I've gone for each type: the rough guy; the nerdy, sweet,
  lovable guy; and the slick guy. I don't really have a type.
  Men in general are a good thing.'

  JENNIFER ANNISTON

• 'Firstly, Tamzin who? Secondly, I think it's disrespectful;
  and thirdly, as if, love.'

  VICTORIA BECKHAM, ON HEARING THAT
  TAMZIN OUTHWAITE WOULDN'T MIND A NIGHT
  WITH HUSBAND DAVID

• 'I fell off my pink cloud with a thud.'

  ELIZABETH TAYLOR

• 'I won't be happy till I'm as famous as God.'

  MADONNA, A LONG TIME AGO

——————— **THINGS CELEBRITIES SAY** ———————

● 'You have to be careful with the clitoris because, if the piercer doesn't know what he's doing, it can be numbed for good.'

JANET JACKSON

● 'Yeah I flirt, I'm not blind and I'm not dead!'

DOLLY PARTON

● 'The FA are still optimistic about England's bid to stage the World Cup in twenty thousand and six.'

PETER SNOW

● 'There is no off position on the genius switch.'

DAVID LETTERMAN

● 'I only get ill when I give up drugs.'

KEITH RICHARDS

● 'I'm rich, freakin' rich. It's crazy.'

BRITNEY SPEARS

● 'I was the first woman to burn my bra – it took the fire department four days to put it out.'

DOLLY PARTON

———— **THINGS CELEBRITIES SAY** ————

● 'I am not the archetypal leading man. This is mainly for one reason: as you may have noticed, I have no hair.'
PATRICK STEWART

● 'The English contribution to world cuisine – the chip.'
JOHN CLEESE

● 'I miss New York. I still love how people talk to you on the street – just assault you and tell you what they think of your jacket.'
MADONNA

● 'I enjoy being a highly overpaid actor.'
ROGER MOORE

● 'If you ever need anything please don't hesitate to ask someone else first.'
KURT COBAIN

● 'Being number two sucks.'
ANDRE AGASSI

● 'Angelina Jolie may get him [Antonio Banderas] in bed for eight hours on a movie set, but I get him in bed every day.'
MELANIE GRIFFITH

THINGS CELEBRITIES SAY

- 'If you want to ask about my drug problem, go ask my big, fat, smart, ten-pound daughter, she'll answer any questions you have about it.'

  COURTNEY LOVE

- 'Being English, I always laugh at anything to do with the lavatory or bottoms.'

  ELIZABETH HURLEY

- 'When I get down on my knees, it is not to pray.'

  MADONNA

- 'I wasn't always black... There was this freckle, and it got bigger and bigger.'

  BILL COSBY

- 'Picasso had his pink period and his blue period. I am in my blonde period right now.'

  HUGH HEFNER

- 'Brad [Pitt], poor geezer, was blown up, thrown around, burned, slapped, frozen. But never a moan or a whine. Now that's what I call a real star.'

  GUY RITCHIE

———— THINGS CELEBRITIES SAY ————

- 'I'm taking my rats. Those are my friends for the tour. Thelma and Louise. They're so cute.'

  PINK

- 'After about 20 years of marriage, I'm finally starting to scratch the surface of that one [what women want]. And I think the answer lies somewhere between conversation and chocolate.'

  MEL GIBSON

- 'Me and Janet really are two different people.'

  MICHAEL JACKSON

- 'Violence is one of the most fun things to watch.'

  QUENTIN TARANTINO

- 'I used to smoke two packs a day and I just hate being a non-smoker... but I will never consider myself a nonsmoker because I always find smokers the most interesting people at the table.'

  MICHELLE PFEIFFER

- 'With two movies opening this summer, I have no relaxing time at all. Whatever I have is spent in a drunken stupor.'

  HUGH GRANT

———— THINGS CELEBRITIES SAY ————

- 'I hope people realise that there is a brain underneath the hair and a heart underneath the boobs.'

  DOLLY PARTON

- 'It was no great tragedy being Judy Garland's daughter. I had tremendously interesting childhood years – except they had little to do with being a child.'

  LIZA MINNELLI

- 'I can't believe people got so upset at the sight of a single breast! America is so parochial, I may just have to move to Europe where people are more mature about things like that!'

  JANET JACKSON

- 'Sometimes you have to be a bitch to get things done.'

  MADONNA

- 'Traffic signals in New York are just rough guidelines.'

  DAVID LETTERMAN

- 'In college I castrated 21 rats, and I got pretty good at it.'

  LISA KUDROW

- 'My favourite thing in the world is a box of fine European chocolates which is, for sure, better than sex.'

  ALICIA SILVERSTONE

--- **THINGS CELEBRITIES SAY** ---

- 'I want a big house with a moat and dragons and a fort to keep people out!'

  VICTORIA BECKHAM

- 'Up until they go to school, they're relatively portable.'

  ELIZABETH HURLEY, ON CHILDREN

- 'Bitches. It's a very male-chauvinist word. I resent it deeply. A person who's a bitch would seem to be mean for no reason. I'm not a mean person. Maybe I'm rude without being aware of it – that's possible.'

  BARBRA STREISAND

- 'If it's hard to remember, it'll be difficult to forget.'

  ARNOLD SCHWARZENEGGER

- 'If I'm in the middle of hitting a most fantastic cross-court back hand top spin and someone says, 'Can you stop now and have sex?' I'll say, "No thanks!"'

  CLIFF RICHARD

- 'Always end the name of your child with a vowel, so that when you yell the name will carry.'

  BILL COSBY

THINGS CELEBRITIES SAY

- 'I don't know much about football. I know what a goal is, which is surely the main thing about football.'

  VICTORIA BECKHAM

- 'Charlton Heston admitted he had a drinking problem, and I said to myself, "Thank God this guy doesn't own any guns!"'

  DAVID LETTERMAN

- 'I've only slept with men I've been married to. How many women can make that claim?'

  ELIZABETH TAYLOR

- 'I knew I was a winner back in the late sixties. I knew I was destined for great things. People will say that kind of thinking is totally immodest. I agree. Modesty is not a word that applies to me in any way – I hope it never will.'

  ARNOLD SCHWARZENEGGER

- 'Cameron Diaz was so cute at the MTV Movie Awards when she pulled her skirt up and wiped her armpits.'

  PINK

- 'Everybody loves you when they are about to come.'

  MADONNA

———————— **THINGS CELEBRITIES SAY** ————————

- 'I look just like the girls next door... if you happen to live next door to an amusement park.'

  DOLLY PARTON

- 'I tell you what really turns my toes up: love scenes with 68-year-old men and actresses young enough to be their granddaughter.'

  MEL GIBSON

- 'I try and take lots of vitamins and I don't drink. I do smoke, though. I'd be insufferable if I didn't smoke, you'd have to push me off a balcony I'd be so boring.'

  KATE BECKINSALE

- 'It's tiny [his butt], what can I do?'

  RICKY MARTIN

- 'I want to die before my wife, and the reason is this: If it is true that when you die, your soul goes up to judgement, I don't want my wife up there ahead of me to tell them things.'

  BILL COSBY

- 'Better to live one year as a tiger, then a hundred as sheep.'

  MADONNA

——— THINGS CELEBRITIES SAY ———

- 'Whatever side I take, I know well that I will be blamed.'
  KEITH RICHARDS

- 'I'm not offended by dumb-blonde jokes because I know
  that I'm not dumb. I also know I'm not blonde.'
  DOLLY PARTON

- 'I veer away from trying to understand why I act. I just
  know I need to do it.'
  RALPH FIENNES

- 'I'm going to marry a Jewish woman because I like
  the idea of getting up Sunday morning and going to
  the deli.'
  MICHAEL J FOX

- 'If it bleeds, we can kill it.'
  ARNOLD SCHWARZENEGGER

- 'You can get Indian food at three in the morning,
  but I personally don't want Indian food at three in the
  morning. I want to go for a walk in my nightgown!'
  ASHLEY JUDD, ON THE PROS AND CONS
  OF LIVING IN NEW YORK

———— **THINGS CELEBRITIES SAY** ————

- 'I'm not used to the C word. That is sort of a new deal. It is so funny. C'mon, I was not raised to take myself that seriously.'

  BRITTANY MURPHY, ON THE NOVELTY OF
  BEING A CELEBRITY

- 'Officially, I am not a woman anymore. Dublin has turned me into a man.'

  KEIRA KNIGHTLEY, ON LEARNING TO DRINK WITH THE BOYS
  WHILE SHE FILMED *KING ARTHUR* IN THE IRISH CAPITAL

- 'All musicians are fun to get drunk with, except the ones who are cleaning up their act. We steer clear of those.'

  ROD STEWART, ON INTOLERANCE FOR LOW TOLERANCE

- 'I didn't pay that much attention to the election. Nobody really grabbed me. The earthquakes in California worry me, so I'm hoping Arnold [Schwarzenegger] might take care of them.'

  DOLLY PARTON, WHO WAS ONCE ASKED TO RUN FOR
  GOVERNOR OF HER NATIVE TENNESSEE

- 'That's the kind of face you hang on your door in Africa.'

  COMEDIENNE JOAN RIVERS, ON PERMA-TANNED FASHION
  QUEEN DONATELLA VERSACE

———— **THINGS CELEBRITIES SAY** ————

● 'He's claiming abuse. I pay my wife good money for a little abuse; a good spanking sometimes. I don't know what he's complaining about.'

CUBA GOODING JR, ON DAVID GEST'S LAWSUIT AGAINST LIZA MINNELLI FOR PHYSICAL ABUSE

● 'In Hollywood now when people die they don't say, "Did he leave a will?" but "Did he leave a diary?"'

LIZA MINNELLI

● 'Health food may be good for the conscience but Oreos taste a hell of a lot better.'

ROBERT REDFORD

● 'Did you ever see the customers in health-food stores? They are pale, skinny people who look half-dead. In a steak house, you see robust, ruddy people. They're dying, of course, but they look terrific.'

BILL COSBY

● 'There are, I think, three countries left in the world where I can go and I'm not as well known as I am here. I'm a pretty big star, folks – I don't have to tell you. Superstar, I guess you could say.'

BRUCE WILLIS

——————— THINGS CELEBRITIES SAY ———————

- 'It was definitely different from kissing a girl. He had a bunch of stray hairs on his lip. The worst part was that we had to do 30 takes.'

  JASON BIGGS, ON LOCKING LIPS WITH SEANN WILLIAM SCOTT IN *AMERICAN WEDDING*

- 'Craig David called me and said he'd written a song based on my song and asked if I'd like to come and sing on it. I asked my son, "Is that cool? Is he cool?", and he was like, "Yes, Dad!", so I said, "Absolutely."'

  STING, ON CAREER ADVICE FROM HIS HIP KIDS

- 'Once you're famous, you realise for the rest of your life sex has to be in the bedroom.'

  SANDRA BULLOCK, ON HER PRE-CELEBRITY SEXUAL TRYST IN A TAXI

- 'I'm so pleased. I couldn't stand any of his stuff. He's always buying me things, but I never let him buy me furniture.'

  SIR ELTON JOHN'S MUM SHEILA, ON HER RELIEF THAT HER SON IS AUCTIONING OFF SOME OF HIS MORE FLAMBOYANT HOME FURNISHINGS

- 'The show was terrible because I didn't win!'

  FRASIER'S DAVID HYDE PIERCE, ON HIS 2003 EMMY AWARD FAILURE

———— THINGS CELEBRITIES SAY ————

- 'We're pleased he doesn't want to listen to the Wiggles –
  he just asks for The Clash.'
  CATE BLANCHETT, ON HER RELIEF THAT HER INFANT SON
  DASHIELL HAS GOOD MUSICAL TASTE

- 'They didn't even shoot my butt. Every now and again,
  you'll see a breast. But, like, big whoops! It's like, have
  you seen an Evian poster lately? Big deal, right?'
  DARYL HANNAH, ON HOW PAINLESS HER
  NUDE PHOTO SHOOT FOR AMERICAN MEN'S
  MAGAZINE *PLAYBOY* WAS

- 'It was a really bad film, I'm really bad in it, and it was
  the hardest thing to go out there and promote it by
  saying, "There are things about this that are fascinating."'
  GEORGE CLOONEY, ON HIS ROLE IN
  BATMAN & ROBIN

- 'People look back on it now with nostalgia and say it
  was great. It was bulls★★★.'
  ROBERT CARLYLE, ON THE 1970S

- 'I have the same goal I've had ever since I was a girl. I
  want to rule the world.'
  MADONNA

THINGS CELEBRITIES SAY

- '*USA Today* has come out with a new survey – apparently, three out of every four people make up 75% of the population.'

  DAVID LETTERMAN

- 'I dress sexily – but not in an obvious way. Sexy in a virginal way.'

  VICTORIA BECKHAM

- 'I used to desire many, many things, but now I have just one desire, and that's to get rid of all my other desires.'

  JOHN CLEESE

- 'I am a survivor. I am like a cockroach, you just can't get rid of me.'

  MADONNA

- 'I would seriously question whether anybody is really foolish enough to really say what they mean. Sometimes I think that civilisation as we know it would kind of break down if we all were completely honest.'

  ELIZABETH HURLEY

- 'The moral of filmmaking in Britain is that you will be screwed by the weather.'

  HUGH GRANT

—————— THINGS CELEBRITIES SAY ——————

● 'It costs a lot of money to look this cheap.'

DOLLY PARTON

● 'I am not going to be no senorita.'

VICTORIA BECKHAM, ON MOVING TO SPAIN

● 'When the sun comes up, I have morals again.'

ELIZABETH TAYLOR

● 'We covered "Hey, Jude". My father panicked, misunderstanding the lyrics and thinking our lead singer was belting out "Hey, Jew" to a roomful of Holocaust survivors.'

BEN STILLER

● 'Wherever we've travelled in this great land of ours, we've found that people everywhere are about 90% water.'

DAVID LETTERMAN

● 'Why does a woman work ten years to change a man's habits and then complain that he's not the man she married?'

BARBRA STREISAND

● 'Passing the vodka bottle. And playing the guitar.'

KEITH RICHARDS, ON HOW HE KEEPS FIT

---------- **THINGS CELEBRITIES SAY** ----------

● 'My parents have been there for me, ever since I was about seven.'

DAVID BECKHAM

● 'People say New Yorkers can't get along. Not true. I saw two New Yorkers, complete strangers, sharing a cab. One guy took the tyres and the radio; the other guy took the engine.'

DAVID LETTERMAN

● 'You know the only people who are always sure about the proper way to raise children? Those who've never had any.'

BILL COSBY

● 'I am my own experiment. I am my own work of art.'

MADONNA

● 'Smoking kills. If you're killed, you've lost a very important part of your life.'

BROOKE SHIELDS

● 'I just use my muscles as a conversation piece, like someone walking a cheetah down 42nd Street.'

ARNOLD SCHWARZENEGGER

——— THINGS CELEBRITIES SAY ———

- 'Old is always 15 years from now.'

  BILL COSBY

- 'I cannot sing, dance or act; what else would I be but a talk-show host.'

  DAVID LETTERMAN

- 'I grew up with a lot of boys. I probably have a lot of testosterone for a woman.'

  CAMERON DIAZ

- 'You're about as useful as a one-legged man at an arse-kicking contest.'

  ROWAN ATKINSON

- 'People have been so busy relating to how I look, it's a miracle I didn't become a self-conscious blob of protoplasm.'

  ROBERT REDFORD

- 'I'm still me even after all that's happened.'

  VICTORIA BECKHAM

- 'New York now leads the world's great cities in the number of people around whom you shouldn't make a sudden move.'

  DAVID LETTERMAN

THINGS CELEBRITIES SAY

- 'The one thing I remember about Christmas was that my father used to take me out in a boat about ten miles offshore on Christmas Day, and I used to have to swim back. Extraordinary. It was a ritual. Mind you, that wasn't the hard part. The difficult bit was getting out of the sack.'

  JOHN CLEESE

- 'My body is like breakfast, lunch, and dinner. I don't think about it, I just have it.'

  ARNOLD SCHWARZENEGGER

- 'There is a new billboard outside Times Square. It keeps an up-to-the-minute count of gun-related crimes in New York. Some goofball is going to shoot someone just to see the numbers move.'

  DAVID LETTERMAN

- 'Human beings are the only creatures on earth that allow their children to come back home.'

  Bill Cosby

- 'You find out who your real friends are when you're involved in a scandal.'

  ELIZABETH TAYLOR

---------- **THINGS CELEBRITIES SAY** ----------

● 'I've always had confidence. Before I was famous, that confidence got me into trouble. After I got famous, it just got me into more trouble.'

BRUCE WILLIS

● 'I always thought I should be treated like a star.'

MADONNA

● 'I'd kill myself if I was as fat as Marilyn Monroe.'

ELIZABETH HURLEY

● 'If someone had told me years ago that sharing a sense of humour was so vital to partnerships, I could have avoided a lot of sex!'

KATE BECKINSALE

● 'If you haven't got it. Fake it! Too short? Wear big high heels. But do practise walking!'

VICTORIA BECKHAM

SPORTS AND GAMES

——————— **SPORTS AND GAMES** ———————

● The only golf course on the island of Tonga has 15 holes, and there's no penalty if a monkey steals your golf ball.

● A US motor racing fan sent more than half a million emails to Fox Entertainment because they'd shown a baseball game instead of a race.

● A gambler won £25,000 by staking £100 on Manchester City to beat Spurs at odds of 250/1 when they were losing 3–0 and down to ten men at half-time.

● Before football referees started using whistles in 1878, they used to rely on waving a handkerchief.

● An experiment at Manchester United showed that David Beckham ran an average 8.8 miles per game – more than any other player in the team.

● If you add up the letters in all the names of the cards in the deck (Ace, two), the total number of letters is 52, the same as the number of cards in the deck.

● Rio Ferdinand was not happy when teammates put yoghurt on his new £200,000 Bentley.

—————— SPORTS AND GAMES ——————

- When the Ancient Greeks played cards, aces were known as 'dogs'.

- Football is the most attended or watched sport in the world.

- Belgian football team FC Wijtschale conceded 58 goals in just two games.

- In the 1988 Calgary Olympics, Eddie 'the Eagle' Edwards finished 58th (last) in the 70m jump and 55th (last) in the 90m.

- The New York Jets were unable to find hotel rooms for a game in Indianapolis recently because they had all been booked up by people attending Gencon, a gaming convention.

- Arsenal stars have been told to stop giving other players their football tops.

- There is a regulation size half-court where employees can play basketball inside the Matterhorn at Disneyland.

- One of baseball pitcher Nolan Ryan's jockstraps recently sold at auction for £13,000.

—————————— **SPORTS AND GAMES** ——————————

- The study of David Beckham is part of a 12-week 'football culture' module for a University Degree course at Staffordshire University.

- A female photographer has been banned from flying with the Romanian soccer team because of superstitions that women could bring bad luck.

- A man from Medellin in Colombia has changed his name to Deportivo Independiente Medellin, after his favourite football team.

- Rio Ferdinand was given a parking ticket because his car was too wide for the parking space. Britain's most expensive footballer fell foul of three wardens when he tried to park his Aston Martin on King Street, in Manchester.

- Another word for volleyball is minonette.

- Chelsea stars are to get a new training-ground aid – a bank of sunbeds.

- The first golf rule booklet was published in Scotland in 1754.

SPORTS AND GAMES

- Tennis pro Evonne Goolagong's last name means 'kangaroo's nose' in Australia's aboriginal language.

- A stringent Real medical revealed that David Beckham has one leg shorter than the other. However, a boot insert to eradicate the problem proved too uncomfortable, so he stopped using it.

- Billiards great Henry Lewis once sank 46 balls in a row.

- Golf great Billy Casper turned golf pro during the Korean War while serving in the Navy. Casper was assigned to operate and build golf driving ranges for the Navy in the San Diego area.

- Norwich City were urged to wear red underpants to help them win a game when they were bottom of the league.

- David Beckham has his wife Victoria's name – albeit misspelled – in Hindi tattooed on his arm. She has 'DB' tattooed on her wrist.

- If you lined up all the slinkys ever made in a row, they could wrap around the Earth 126 times.

SPORTS AND GAMES

● Not all golf balls have 360 dimples. There are some as high as 420. There are also many different kinds of dimple patterns.

● In July 1934, Babe Ruth paid a fan $20 dollars for the return of the baseball he hit for his 700th career home run.

● In 1969, a brief battle broke out between Honduras and El Salvador. Although tensions had been rough between the two countries, the reason for the war was El Salvador's victory over Honduras in the World Cup football playoffs. Gunfire was exchanged for about 30 minutes before reason could prevail.

● David Beckham says he is not a beer drinker, and prefers a nice glass of wine or Pepsi.

● Horseracing is one of the most dangerous sports. Between two and three jockeys are killed each year. That's about how many baseball players have died in baseball's entire professional history.

● Michael Owen has joked that he likes wearing tights in the privacy of his own home.

—————— SPORTS AND GAMES ——————

- America's national sport of baseball was mentioned in a novel by Jane Austen.

- Gene Sarazen, a golfer from several generations ago, set the record for the fastest golf drive: 120mph.

- Michael Sangster, who played in the 1960s, had tennis' fastest serve, once clocked at 154mph.

- In 1964, for the 10th time in his major-league baseball career, Mickey Mantle hit home runs from both the left and right sides of the plate in the same game – setting a new baseball record.

- Footballer David Beckham and with pop star wife Victoria are said to be worth a combined £50 million.

- The late Pope John Paul II was named an 'Honorary Harlem Globetrotter' in 2000.

- More money is spent on gardening than any other hobby.

- In a TV poll at the end of 2003, David Beckham was voted the fifth most popular 'Spaniard'. Experts said people had not understood the question properly.

SPORTS AND GAMES

- A north-west cricket club held a minute's silence to remember a dead club member only to later find out he was alive.

- Former world chess champion Ruslan Ponomariov has become the first player to be disqualified at a major event after his mobile phone rang during a game.

- Goran Ivanisevic's father crashed his £2 million yacht, not long after a friend wrote off his £100,000 Porsche.

- The pitches that baseball player Babe Ruth hit for his last-ever home run and that Joe DiMaggio hit for his first-ever home run were thrown by the same man.

- The national sport of Nauru, a small Pacific island, is lassoing flying birds.

- David Beckham's father missed his son's home debut for Real Madrid after losing his passport.

- The 'huddle' in American football was formed because of a deaf football player who used sign language to communicate and his team didn't want the opposition to see the signals he used and in turn huddled around him.

SPORTS AND GAMES

- When a male skier falls down, he tends to fall on his face. A woman skier tends to fall on her back.

- Tiger Woods is the only person to hold all four major championships at one time, although it did not happen in the calendar year. He also currently holds the scoring record for all four majors.

- Tony Hawk has made more money from video games and TV commercials than from skateboarding.

- David Beckham wears a new pair of football boots for every game he plays at an estimated cost of £300 a pair.

- Men are a lot more streamlined than women for swimming, because the female's mammaries create a lot of drag, enough, in fact, that racing suits have been developed with tiny pegs above the breasts to cause disturbance, which decreases the drag.

- Steven Gerrard's fiancée arrived in Portugal not knowing who England were playing in their first match of Euro 2004.

- Sainsbury's minted Euro 2004 medals engraved with the names and pictures of three players not in the England squad.

SPORTS AND GAMES

- 'Vaimonkanto' or 'wife carrying' is a sports event. The championship games are held annually in Sonkajarvi, Finland.

- Enthusiasts of a 'sport' called extreme ironing are trying to get Olympic recognition by going to the US to show off their skills in ironing in extreme places like Times Square and Mount Rushmore.

- David Beckham's weekly wage is reported to be anything between £90,000 and £120,000.

- Around 18 million more text messages than normal were sent on the day England clinched victory against Australia in the Rugby World Cup final.

- In the 1870s, William Russell Frisbie opened a bakery called the Frisbie Pie Company in Bridgeport, Connecticut. His lightweight pie tins were embossed with the family name. In the mid-1940s, students at Yale University tossed the empty pie tins as a game.

- In the United States, more Frisbee discs are sold each year than baseballs, basketballs and footballs combined.

- Ernie Els's real name is Theodore.

———————— SPORTS AND GAMES ————————

- Go-karting started in the mid-1950s and was originally considered to be a fad.

- 'Hot cockles' was a popular game at Christmas in medieval times. Players took turns striking a blindfolded player, who had to guess the name of the person delivering each blow.

- There are more recreational golfers per capita in Canada than any other country in the world.

- The longest monopoly game in a bathtub is 99 hours.

- On 21 February 2004, over 1,500 minor hockey players gathered along Ottawa's 7.8km Rideau Canal for 110 simultaneous games of hockey.

- Daniele Carassai, manager of semi-professional side Gotico, was sacked by a text message saying 'You're sacked'.

- Scarborough goalie Leigh Walker was 'sickened' after his mother washed a Chelsea shirt that had been signed by all the team.

- Brazilian soccer star Ronaldinho smashed a window at a 12th-century cathedral after fluffing an overhead kick while filming an advert.

SPORTS AND GAMES

- Camden playground in Janesville, Wisconsin is the largest handicapped-accessible playground in the world.

- At 101, Larry Lewis ran the 100-yard dash in 17.8 seconds setting a new world record for runners 100 years old or older.

- A helicopter installed the world's largest Olympic torch on top of the Calgary tower. The flame was visible for 15–20km and required 30,000 cubic feet of natural gas/hour.

- Johnny Plessey batted .331 for the Cleveland Spiders in 1891, even though he spent the entire season batting with a rolled-up, lacquered copy of the Toledo *Post-Dispatch*.

- The average IQ of a WWF fan is 83, roughly 17 points below the national average.

- When the golf ball was introduced in 1848, it was called a 'gutta-percha'.

- To bulk up, sumo wrestlers eat huge portions of protein-rich stews called chankonabe, packed with fish or meat and vegetables, plus vast quantities of less healthy foods, including fast food. They often force themselves to eat

—————— SPORTS AND GAMES ——————

when they are full, and they have a nap after lunch, thus acquiring flab on top of their strong muscles, which helps to keep their centre of gravity low.

- The chances of making two holes-in-one in a round of golf are one in 67 million.

- If placed end-to-end, all Lego sets sold during the past ten years would stretch from London, UK, to Perth, Australia.

- In 1974, Bob Chandler built the first monster truck – Bigfoot – his dream truck, a four-wheel drive Ford F-250 with a jacked-up suspension and oversized tyres.

- In 1988, the heaviest sumo wrestler ever recorded weighed in at a thundering 560lb.

- Table tennis was originally played with balls made from champagne corks and paddles made from cigar-box lids.

TECHNOLOGY
AND SCIENCE

─────── **TECHNOLOGY AND SCIENCE** ───────

- An employee of the Alabama Department of Transportation installed spyware on his boss's computer and proved that the boss spent 10% of his time working, 20% of time checking stocks and 70% of the time playing solitaire. The employee was fired, but the boss kept his job.

- Physicists have already performed a simple type of teleportation, transferring the quantum characteristics of one atom on to another atom at a different location.

- A German supermarket chain has introduced a new way of allowing customers to pay using just their fingerprints.

- The annual growth of WWW traffic is 314,000%.

- James Dyson has invented a vacuum cleaner that can order its own spare parts.

- The 'save' icon on Microsoft Word shows a floppy disk, with the shutter on backwards.

- Thirty-two per cent of singles polled think they will meet their future mate online.

- Scientists have performed a surgical operation on a single living cell, using a needle that is just a few millionths of a metre wide.

—————— **TECHNOLOGY AND SCIENCE** ——————

● As much as 80% of microwaves from mobile phones are said to be absorbed by your head.

● Thomas Edison designed a helicopter that would work with gunpowder. It exploded and also blew up his factory.

● An x-ray security scanner that sees through people's clothes has been deployed at Heathrow Airport.

● The last time an astronaut walked on the moon was in 1979.

● The time spent deleting SPAM costs United States businesses £11.2 billion annually.

● A remote tribe in the Brazilian jungle are now online after a charity gave them five battery-powered computers.

● The cruise liner *Queen Elizabeth II* burns a gallon of diesel for each 6in that it moves.

● The Church of England has appointed its first web pastor to oversee a new parish that will exist only on the net.

──── TECHNOLOGY AND SCIENCE ────

- The light from your computer monitor streams at you at almost 186,000 miles a second.

- More than 50% of the people in the world have never made or received a telephone call.

- 35 billion emails are sent each day throughout the world.

- Insurance company Esure announced plans to use voice stress analysis technology to weed out fraudulent claims.

- The screwdriver was invented before the screw.

- Scientists in Australia have developed software that allows people to log on to PCs by laughing.

- The first meal eaten on the moon by Neil Armstrong and Buzz Aldrin was cold roast turkey and trimmings.

- The newest trend in the Netherlands is having tiny jewels implanted directly into the eye.

- Researchers have found that doctors who spend at least three hours a week playing video games make about 37% fewer mistakes in laparoscopic surgery than surgeons who didn't play video games.

———— TECHNOLOGY AND SCIENCE ————

- The first domain name ever registered was Symbolics.com.

- Every single 'all-a' domain name, from a.com to aaaaaaaaaaaaaaaaaaaaaaaaaaaaaaaaaaaaaaaaaaaaaaaaaaaaaaaaa aaaaaa.com (63 as), has been registered.

- Every single possible 3-character .com domain (over 50,000) has long since been registered!

- Bill Gates was once an employee for Apple.

- The highest publicly reported amount of money paid for a domain name is £3.9 million, paid for business.com.

- A single individual, Dr Lieven P Van Neste, owns over 200,000 domain names.

- Every five seconds a computer is infected with a virus.

- The first personal computer was called the Altair and was made by a company called MITS in 1974. It came in a kit and had to be assembled by the user.

- IBM introduced their first personal computer in 1981.

TECHNOLOGY AND SCIENCE

- The basis of the Macintosh computer was Apple's Lisa, which was released in 1983. This was the first system to utilise a GUI or Graphical User Interface. The first Macintosh was released in 1984.

- The name 'Intel' stems from the company's former name, 'Integrated Electronics'.

- Over 23% of all photocopier faults worldwide are caused by people sitting on them and photocopying their bottoms.

- The town of Halfway, Oregon, temporarily changed its name to half.com as a publicity stunt for the website of the same name.

- Scandinavia leads the world in internet access according to the UN communications agency.

- Hornby has invented a way of connecting a Scalextric track to a PC so people can race each other on the internet.

- Readers of the technical innovation website T3.co.uk have voted the widget as the greatest technological invention in 40 years.

—— TECHNOLOGY AND SCIENCE ——

- The first scheme in the UK which allows drivers to pay for parking by mobile phone was launched in Scotland.

- The telescope on Mount Palomar, California, can see a distance of 7,038,835,200,000,000 million miles.

- PlayStation2 game WWE SmackDown: Here Comes The Pain features female competitors trying to rip each other's clothes off.

- Britney Spears, Harry Potter and The Matrix topped the list of the most frequently searched subjects in 2003 on Google.

- A Belgian couple got married by SMS because text messaging played such a big part in their relationship.

- In February 2002, friends reunited was in the top-ten most visited websites in the UK.

- In April 2003, the total number of registered friends reunited members was 8.6 million.

- Twenty-seven per cent of all web transactions are abandoned at the payment screen.

- Four out of five visitors never come back to a website.

———— **TECHNOLOGY AND SCIENCE** ————

- Space on a big company's homepage is worth about 1,300 times as much as land in the business districts of Tokyo.

- The typewriter was invented before the fountain pen.

- Monster truck engines are custom-built, alcohol-injected and usually cost around $35,000. They burn 2–2.5 gallons of methanol per run (approx. 250ft).

- 1,314 phone calls are misplaced by telecom services every minute.

- According to research, Britons collectively make 132 million mobile-phone calls a day.

- A plane that flies without fuel by riding on a ground-based laser beam has been successfully tested by scientists.

- Airbags are deployed at a rate of 200mph.

- Two very popular and common objects have the same function, but one has thousands of moving parts, while the other has absolutely no moving parts – an hourglass and a sundial.

———— **TECHNOLOGY AND SCIENCE** ————

- Russian scientists have developed a new drug that prolongs drunkenness and enhances intoxication.

- The fish reel was invented around 300 AD.

- An ounce of gold can be stretched into a wire 50 miles long.

- Spam filters that catch the word 'cialis' will not allow many work-related emails through because that word is embedded inside the word 'specialist'.

- Orange and DaimlerChrysler UK joined forces to launch the UK's first car that comes with an integrated handsfree phone system.

- There are 150,000,000 mobile phones in use in the United States, more than one for every two human beings in the country.

- A Boeing 767 airliner is made of 3,100,000 separate parts.

- Replying more than 100 times to the same piece of spam e-mail will overwhelm the sender's system and interfere with their ability to send any more spam.

——— TECHNOLOGY AND SCIENCE ———

- A person sneezing was the first thing Thomas Edison filmed with his movie camera.

- A German company has built the world's first washing machine that talks and recognises spoken commands.

- Telecom provider Telewest Broadband is testing a device that hooks to your PC and wafts a scent when certain emails arrive.

- The Air Force's F-117 fighter uses aerodynamics discovered during research into how bumblebees fly.

- Silly Putty was 'discovered' as the residue left behind after the first latex condoms were produced. It's not widely publicised for obvious reasons.

- The largest thing ever built was the Grand Coulee dam. Three times the bulk of the bouler dam and four times the volume of the Great Pyramid, nearly a mile long and 550ft high. Its 30-acre base was 500ft wide and held back the Columbia River. It consumed 12 million cubic yards of concrete.

- The Mars Rover 'Spirit' is powered by six small motors the size of 'C' batteries. It has a top speed of 0.1mph.

———— TECHNOLOGY AND SCIENCE ————

- Bulletproof vests, fire escapes, windshield wipers and laser printers were all invented by women.

- The Oblivion ride at Alton Towers has a G-force of 5. That's higher than the G-force of an average NASA take-off!

NATURAL
SCIENCE

—————— NATURAL SCIENCE ——————

- It took approximately 2.5 million blocks to build the Pyramid of Giza, which is one of the Great Pyramids.

- Each year, 16 million gallons of oil run off pavements into streams, rivers and eventually oceans in the United States. This is more oil than was spilled by the Exxon Valdez.

- The Earth is turning to desert at a rate of 40 square miles per day.

- Orthodox rabbis warned that New York City drinking water might not be kosher; it contains harmless micro-organisms that are technically shellfish.

- There are more stars than all of the grains of sand on earth.

- The Netherlands has built 800 miles of massive dykes and sea walls to hold back the sea.

- Twenty per cent of the earth's surface is permanently frozen.

- The rain in New York carries so much acid from pollution that it has killed all the fish in 200 lakes in the Adirondack State Park.

NATURAL SCIENCE

- All humans are 99.9% genetically identical and 98.4% of human genes are the same as the genes of a chimpanzee.

- Natural gas has no odour. The smell is added artificially so that leaks can be detected.

- The magnetic North Pole shifts by about 7m a day.

- In 1783, an Icelandic eruption threw up enough dust to temporarily block out the sun over Europe.

- A huge underground river runs underneath the Nile, with six times more water than the river above.

- A day on the planet Mercury is twice as long as its year.

- Mexico City sinks about 10in a year.

- Two to four million tons of oil leak into the Soviet water table every year from the Siberian pipeline.

- The dioxin 2,3,7,8-tetrachlorodibenzo-p-dioxin is 150,000 times deadlier than cyanide.

- Some large clouds store enough water for 500,000 showers.

─────────── NATURAL SCIENCE ───────────

- There is an average of two earthquakes every minute in the world.

- After billions of years, black holes become white holes and they spit out all the things they sucked up.

- Siberia contains more than 25% of the world's forests.

- The world's windiest place is Commonwealth Bay, Antartica.

- Half of all forest fires are started by lightning.

- It is said the average person speaks only ten minutes a day.

- Due to gravitational effects, you weigh slightly less when the moon is directly overhead.

- The only rock that floats in water is pumice.

- The most abundant metal in the Earth's crust is aluminium.

- Plants that are not cared for will cry for help; a thirsty plant will make a high-pitched sound that is too high for us to hear.

———————— NATURAL SCIENCE ————————

- Seawater, loaded with mineral salts, weighs about a pound and a half more per cubit foot than fresh water at the same temperature.

- If you were to count off 1 billion seconds, it would take you 31.7 years.

- If you disassembled the Great Pyramid of Cheops, you would get enough stones to encircle the earth with a brick wall 20 inches high.

- Electricity doesn't move through a wire but through a field around the wire.

- The Earth is not round, but slightly pear-shaped.

- Six of the seven continents can grow pumpkins [even Alaska can]. Antarctica is the only continent where they won't grow.

- It can take up to 15 years for a Christmas tree to grow, but on average, it takes about seven years.

- Myrrh is a plant oil used to bury the dead and a symbol of mortality.

--------------- **NATURAL SCIENCE** ---------------

- The size of a raindrop is around 0.5mm–2.5mm, and they fall from the sky on average 21 feet per second.

- Sound carries so well in the Arctic that, on a calm day, a conversation can be heard from 1.8 miles away.

- Sleet is a form of snow that begins to fall, but melts on its way down.

- The large number of reflecting surfaces of the crystal makes snow appear white.

- Partly melted ice crystals usually cling together to form snowflakes, which may in rare cases grow in size up to 3 to 4in in diameter.

- If a person were to ask what is the most northern point in the United States, the most southern point in the United States, and so on, three of the four compass directions are located in Alaska: North East and West.

- A small child could crawl through a blue whale's major arteries.

- The planet Saturn has a density lower than water so, if there was a bathtub large enough to hold it, Saturn would float.

NATURAL SCIENCE

- After the Krakatoa volcano eruption in 1883 in Indonesia, many people reported that, because of the dust, the sunset appeared green and the moon blue.

- If you are standing on a mountain top and the conditions are just right, you can see a lit match from 50 miles away.

- The gnomon is the thing that casts the shadow on a sundial.

- The biggest crystals in the world are found in a silver mine in Mexico, The Cave of Crystals. They are made of gypsum , some of which are 12 meters long.

- The Cullinan Diamond is the largest gem-quality diamond ever discovered. Found in 1905, the original 3,100 carats were cut to make jewels for the British Crown Jewels and the British Royal family's collection.

- The fastest shooting stars travel at 150,000mph.

- When you look at the full moon, what you see is only one fifth the size of the continent of Africa.

NATURAL SCIENCE

- A coalmine fire in Haas Canyon, Colorado, was ignited by spontaneous combustion in 1916 and withstood all efforts to put it out. The 900-1700° fire was eventually quenched by a heat-resistant foam mixed with grout in 2000.

- An iceberg the size of Long Island, New York, broke off Antarctica and blocked sea lanes used by both ships and penguins.

- The winter of 1932 was so cold that Niagara Falls froze completely solid.

- In 2003, there were 86 days of below-freezing weather in Hell, Michigan.

- Plants can suffer from jet lag.

- The Eiffel Tower shrinks 6 inches in winter.

- A snowflake can take up to an hour to fall from the cloud to the surface of the Earth.

- Only 5% of the ocean floor has been mapped in as much detail as the surface of Mars.

―――――――――― **NATURAL SCIENCE** ――――――――――

• Urea is found in human urine and Dalmatian dogs and nowhere else.

• Humans have dammed up over 10 trillion gallons of water over the last four decades.

• In spring, the melting dome of an igloo is replaced with a covering of animal skins to form a between-season dwelling called a 'qarmaq'.

• 1% of the land area in the US has been hit by tornadoes in the last 100 years.

• It is estimated that 10,000,000,000,000,000,000,000,000,000,000,000,000 snowflakes have fallen to the Earth since it was formed.

• In Gabon, there are several 1.8 billion-year-old natural nuclear reactors.

• Lightning strikes about 6,000 times per minute on this planet.

• It is impossible for a solar eclipse to last for more than seven minutes 58 seconds.

NATURAL SCIENCE

- In Montana, in 1887, the largest snowflakes on record fell to the earth. Each snowflake was 15 inches in diameter.

POLITICS

—————————— **POLITICS** ——————————

- Jimmy Carter once reported a UFO in Georgia.

- Texas is the only state that permits residents to cast absentee ballots from space.

- Almost 20% of the billions of dollars American taxpayers are spending to rebuild Iraq are lost to theft, kickbacks and corruption.

- The fertility rate in states that voted for George Bush is 12% higher than states that favoured John Kerry.

- The US Treasury Department has more than 20 people assigned to catching people who violate the trade and tourism embargo with Cuba. In contrast, it has only four employees assigned to track the assets of Osama Bin Ladin and Saddam Hussein.

- More than 8,100 US troops are still listed as missing in action from the Korean War.

- There are 68,000 miles of phone line in the Pentagon.

- George W Bush and John Kerry are 16th cousins, three times removed.

POLITICS

- Legislators in Santa Fe, New Mexico, are considering a law that would require pets to wear seat belts when travelling in a car.

- As of January 2004, the United States economy borrows £780,000,000 each day from foreign investors.

- During Bill Clinton's entire eight-year presidency, he only sent two emails. One was to John Glenn when he was aboard the space shuttle, and the other was a test of the email system.

- In 2004, 60.7% of eligible voters participated in the US presidential election, the highest percentage in 36 years. However, more than 78 million did not vote. This means President Bush won re-election by receiving votes from less than 31% of all eligible voters in the United States.

- CNN's coverage of John Kerry's acceptance speech at the Democratic Convention was marred by the accidental broadcast of expletives from a technician.

- Stalin was only five feet, four inches tall.

- Charles Kennedy's Liberal Democrats committed an embarrassing blunder by accidentally emailing election plans to opponents.

POLITICS

- The First Minister of the Welsh Assembly was mistaken for a *Doctor Who* villain. BBC staff thought Rhodri Morgan was an actor set to play a treelike monster on the sci-fi show.

- Norway's Crown Prince Haakon placed Portugal on the Mediterranean in a welcome speech for the country's president.

- The day after President George W Bush was re-elected, Canada's main immigration website had 115,000 visitors. Before Bush's re-election, this site averaged about 20,000 visitors each day.

- Greek officials had to apologise after dropping a 113-year-old man from an electoral register because they refused to believe he was still alive.

- Cherie Blair began her controversial tour Down Under by calling her Kiwi hosts Australians.

- A Staffordshire county councillor who used civic funds to buy police a mobile speed camera was caught speeding by the same camera.

POLITICS

- A war veteran who got lost on his way back from the D-Day commemorations got a lift back to Paris from French President Jacques Chirac.

- About 1,600 Belgians turned out to vote in the country's elections wearing only swimming costumes or trunks.

- Benjamin Franklin gave guitar lessons.

- The Pentagon now has twice as many bathrooms as when it was built in the 1940s.

- John Kerry's hometown newspaper, the *Lowell Sun*, endorsed George W Bush for president. Bush's hometown newspaper, the *Lone Star Iconoclast*, endorsed John Kerry for president.

- George W Bush, who presents himself as a man of faith, rarely goes to church. Yet he won nearly two out of three voters who attend church at least once a week.

- An NHS patient has become the holder of the new world record for the longest wait on a hospital trolley. Tony Collins spent 77 hours and 30 minutes waiting for treatment.

-------------------------------- POLITICS --------------------------------

- The oldest person to ever be issued a driver's licence in the US was 109.

- All radios in North Korea have been rigged so listeners can only receive a North Korean government station. The United States recently announced plans to smuggle £1,000,000 worth of small radios into the country so North Koreans can get a taste of (what their government calls) 'rotten imperialist reactionary culture'.

- George Washington spent about 7% of his annual salary on liquor.

- The French government has banned the use of the word 'email' in all its ministries, documents, publications and websites.

- Norwegian MP Trond Helleland was caught playing games on his handheld computer during a debate in Parliament.

- A Brazilian MP lost his seat over allegations that he offered voters free Viagra in exchange for their support.

- India has an estimated 550 million voters.

POLITICS

- UK Conservative MP John Bercow sold his 18th-century home because his long-legged fiancée kept bumping her head on the low ceilings.

- The New York City Police Department has a £1.7 billion annual budget, larger than all but 19 of the world's armies.

- Television stations hung banners at the 2004 Democratic National Convention, including Al-Jazeera, until it was noticed and taken down.

- So far, the US Congress has authorised £79,500,000,000 for the Iraq War. This is enough to build over 17,500 elementary schools.

- The US House of Representatives earmarked £26,000,000 to create an indoor rain forest in Iowa.

- The Oval Office is only 22ft long.

- In an effort to encourage the use of nuclear energy, the United States lent highly enriched uranium to countries all over the world between 1950 and 1988. Enough weapons-grade material to make 1,000 nuclear bombs has still not been returned by such countries as Pakistan, Iran, Israel and South Africa.

CRIME AND
CRIMINALS

———— **CRIME AND POLITICS** ————

- You can be imprisoned for not voting in Fiji, Chile and Egypt – at least in theory.

- 0.7% of Americans are currently in prison.

- Frank Wathernam was the last prisoner to leave Alcatraz Prison on 21 March 1963.

- Quebec City, Canada, has about as much street crime as Disney World.

- Police in Finland have issued a £116,000 fine to a man who was caught exceeding a 25mph speed limit.

- An Argentinean burglar who got stuck in a chimney was ordered to rebuild it himself.

- Russian police stopped women drivers to hand out flowers instead of speeding tickets to mark International Women's Day.

- The average length for a criminal sentence in Colombia is 137 years.

- Police officers in India have invited the public to post jokes about them in a bid to improve the image of the force.

—————— **CRIME AND CRIMINALS** ——————

- Two-thirds of the world's kidnappings occur in Colombia.

- Al Capone's older brother Vince was a policeman in Nebraska.

- A drug-sniffer dog working at a UK prison has received death threats because it's so good at its job.

- More than 400 policemen in a Mexican city have been ordered to go on a diet.

- A German man faced up to ten years in a Turkish prison because his nine-year-old son picked up pebbles from a beach. He was charged with smuggling archaeologically valuable national treasures.

- A Czech prisoner locked up on theft charges was freed and allowed to go back home to his wife after getting a permanent erection.

- A robber was jailed for 12 years in Illinois – despite singing to the court in an effort to get a reduced sentence.

- America puts more of its citizens in prison than any other nation.

——————— CRIME AND POLITICS ———————

- An Argentinean man was cleared of urinating on the steps of a museum because they were already dirty.

- The average number of cars stolen per day in Mexico City is 124.

- Police are investigating after a magician's rabbit was 'liberated' mid-act by a suspected animal-rights activist in Brighton.

- The prisoners of a small Brazilian jail are paying the bills in exchange for better conditions.

- The United States has 5% of the world's population, but 25% of the world's prison population.

- An Indian police chief is asking bank managers to feed stray dogs to encourage them to guard their premises.

- Two-thirds of the world's executions occur in China.

- British customs officers have arrested an air passenger carrying more than her own weight in edible snails.

- Post office staff in Malaysia once found 21,000 undelivered letters stored in an apartment that used to be rented out by one of their colleagues.

────── CRIME AND CRIMINALS ──────

- A Texas prisoner who threw his faeces over a prison officer has been given an additional 50 years in prison for harassment.

- Germany has drawn up blueprints for Europe's first jail specifically to house OAPs – old-aged prisoners.

- Classical music and aromatherapy are being used in a Mexican jail to try to calm down some of the most dangerous prisoners.

- The Belgium news agency Belga reported that a man suspected of robbing a jewellery store in Liege said he couldn't have done it because he was busy breaking into a school at the same time. Police then arrested him for breaking into the school.

- A couple caught on camera robbing a store could not be identified until the police reviewed the security tape. The woman had filled out an entry form for a free trip prior to robbing the store.

- A man was arrested and charged with the robbery of vending machines. The man posted his bail entirely in quarters.

——————— CRIME AND POLITICS ———————

- A Romanian man jailed four years earlier for burgling a wealthy neighbour's flat was caught by the same policeman robbing the same property hours after he was released from jail.

- In a stroke of irony, the maximum-security prison in St Albans, Vermont, was responsible in 1996 for sending out public-relations brochures enticing tourists to visit Vermont.

- Airport security personnel find about six weapons a day searching passengers.

- Wayne Black, a suspected thief, had his name tattooed across his forehead. When confronted by police, Black insisted he wasn't Wayne Black. To prove it, he stood in front of a mirror and insisted he was Kcalb Enyaw.

- Overweight policemen in the Philippines have been ordered to take an anti-obesity drug to help the force slim down.

- A Bolivian man spent two months in jail charged with smuggling cocaine before tests revealed he had in fact been carrying talcum powder.

——————CRIME AND CRIMINALS——————

- In Texas, a recently passed anticrime law requires criminals to give their victims 24 hours' notice, either orally or in writing, and to explain the nature of the crime to be committed.

- A gentleman mugger in Austria has been jailed despite his elderly victim's pleas for him to be let off because he was so polite.

- The prison system is the largest supplier of mental-health services in America, with 250,000 Americans with mental illness living there.

- In Bangladesh, kids as young as 15 can be jailed for cheating in their finals.

- Former enemies America and Russia now have a great deal in common – they both lead the world in locking people up.

- You're 66 times more likely to be prosecuted in the USA than in France.

- The Chico, California, City Council enacted a ban on nuclear weapons, setting a £300 fine for anyone detonating one within city limits.

CRIME AND POLITICS

- In September 2004, a Minnesota state trooper issued a speeding ticket to a motorcyclist who was clocked at 205mph.

- A Chinese truck driver has been arrested for kidnapping two toll station operators to save the equivalent of 70 pence.

- In Ancient Egypt, killing a cat was a crime punishable by death.

- In Hong Kong, a betrayed wife is legally allowed to kill her adulterous husband, but may only do so with her bare hands.

- Men in Costa Rica can now be sent to prison for trying to chat up women.

- Russians reportedly pay out more than £19 billion a year in bribes, with the average person paying almost a tenth of their wages in bribes.

- In Ancient Greece, an adulterous male was sometimes punished by the removal of his pubic hair and the insertion of a large radish into his rectum.

CRIME AND CRIMINALS

- In Alaska, it is legal to shoot bears. However, waking a sleeping bear for the purpose of taking a photograph is prohibited.

- A drunken German who bought three hand grenades at a flea market in Bosnia has been arrested after throwing one out of the window to see whether it worked.

- Duelling is legal in Paraguay as long as both parties are registered blood donors.

- Police in Canada impounded an ambulance after arresting the driver for trying to pick up a prostitute.

- It is a criminal offence to drive around in a dirty car in Russia.

- A prisoner in Decatur, Georgia, fell through the roof of a courthouse and into a judge's chambers while trying to escape.

- A woman was chewing what was left of her chocolate bar when she entered a Metro station in Washington DC. She was arrested and handcuffed; eating is prohibited in Metro stations.

CRIME AND POLITICS

- A sketch of a burglar drawn by an 11-year-old schoolboy was so good it allowed Austrian police to catch the thief less than an hour later.

- Four jails in Brazil are using geese to help prevent prisoners from escaping.

- To help reduce budget deficits, several states have begun reducing the amount of food served to prison inmates. In Texas, the number of daily calories served to prisoners was cut by 300, saving the state £3,000,000 per year.

- Hondas and Toyotas are the most frequently stolen passenger cars because they have parts that can be readily exchanged between model years without a problem.

ENTERTAINMENT

ENTERTAINMENT

- Marilyn Monroe had six toes on one foot. ✓

- Actor Bill Murray doesn't have a publicist or an agent.

- During *The Empire Strikes Back*'s famous asteroid scene, one of the deadly hurling asteroids is actually a potato.

- Rocker Ozzy Osbourne has had two smiley face tattoos etched on his kneecaps so he can talk to them when he's feeling lonely.

- Oasis singer Liam Gallagher has received the top prize in *Nuts* magazine's 'man boobs' awards.

- The sound effect for the light sabres in *Star Wars* was recorded by moving a microphone next to a television set.

- In 1979, Oscar-winning actress Shirley MacLaine used the podium to cheer up her sibling, Warren Beatty, who had lost out for *Heaven Can Wait*. 'I want to use this opportunity to say how proud I am of my little brother. Just imagine what you could accomplish if you tried celibacy!' He was not amused.

- A low-cut gown worn by Elizabeth Taylor in 1969 fetched £98,000 at auction.

ENTERTAINMENT

- The youngest actor to win an Oscar was 29-year-old Adrien Brody in 2003 for *The Pianist*. Shirley Temple is the youngest actress. She won a special award in 1934 aged six.

- The song 'When Irish Eyes Are Smiling' was written by ✓ George Graff, who was German and was never in Ireland in his life.

- Talk-show queen Oprah Winfrey and legendary singer Elvis Presley are distant cousins.

- The estates of 22 dead celebrities earned over £2.6 million in 2004. These celebrities include Elvis Presley, Dr Seuss, Charles Schulz, J R R Tolkien and John Lennon.

- CBS's fine for Janet Jackson's 'wardrobe malfunction' in the 2004 Super Bowl show was £286,000. This could be paid with only 7.5 seconds of commercial time during the same Super Bowl telecast.

- *Kill Bill* star Vivica A Fox ruined a diamond-encrusted dress worth $1.5 million with red wine.

- In 1938, Walt Disney won one full-sized Oscar and seven miniature Oscars for his classic *Snow White and the Seven Dwarfs*.

ENTERTAINMENT

- Actor Gary Lucy thought he had paid £6,000 for one of Paul Weller's guitars at an auction, but got rugs belonging to Madonna instead.

- Nicole Kidman says when she was younger she used to pray she would be turned into a witch.

- Al Gore's roommate in college (Harvard, class of 1969) was Tommy Lee Jones.

- The trucking company Elvis Presley worked at as a young man was owned by Frank Sinatra.

- Lenny Kravitz says he's happy Courtney Love is his neighbour – because she runs around naked.

- Britney Spears has more hate websites than Saddam Hussein.

- Calvin Klein model-turned-actor Travis Fimmel had to audition nine times before landing the title role in the new TV series *Tarzan*.

- Three Oscars have been refused by winners, including Marlon Brando in 1972, who rejected his second Oscar for *The Godfather*.

ENTERTAINMENT

- Pop hunk Justin Timberlake's links with McDonald's have paid off for the fast-food chain – profits are up 12% since the *NSYNC star started endorsing the company by letting them use his 'I'm Lovin' It' tune for TV commercials.

- The Strokes star Nikolai Fraiture once shamed his dad when he was caught trying to steal a Luke Skywalker doll from the Macy's store where his father worked as a security guard.

- Actress Rosie O'Donnell's lover Kelli Carpenter has founded a new travel company that helps gay and lesbian couples seek out the perfect getaway. R Family Vacations will specialise in gay cruises.

- US singer Shania Twain has started the day off the same way for the past ten years – with a fruit smoothie made with grapes and ginger.

- Posh frocks at the Oscars can mean huge publicity for designers. Valentino estimated that *Erin Brockovich* star Julia Roberts's appearance in one of his designs generated some £13 million worth of publicity.

——————— ENTERTAINMENT ———————

- Jet-setting pop svengali Simon Fuller, creator of *Pop Idol*, spent £9 million on two aeroplanes and a helicopter because he was sick of flying 90,000 miles a year on commercial airlines.

- Hollywood veteran Jack Nicholson has become addicted to baked beans on toast. The *Anger Management* star discovered the snack after serving it up to 12-year-old son Raymond.

- Malnourished magician David Blaine's first public meal after his self-imposed 44-day incarceration in a plastic box was a plate of chicken satay at Mr Chow's restaurant in Knightsbridge, London. He followed this with a big helping of dessert.

- Former basketball ace Dennis Rodman claims the police have visited his Newport Beach, California, home over 80 times because of noise complaints.

- The first Oscar went to Emil Jannings in 1929 for Best Actor. He didn't turn up for it.

- Dennis Rodman also claims he's pierced his penis three times.

ENTERTAINMENT

- The Strokes star Julian Casablancas doesn't own a mobile phone, a computer or a watch.

- During a one-day shopping spree in Japan, US rapper Lil Kim spent £25,000 on clothes – and Barbie dolls.

- Hollywood stars Demi Moore and Ashton Kutcher spent the Halloween of 2003 dressed as rival supercouple Jennifer Lopez and Ben Affleck.

- Model-turned-actress Jerry Hall has appeared on stage 536 times in plays.

- It takes 12 people 20 hours to make one Oscar statuette.

- Indie rockers Coldplay like to keep in touch with their family and friends when they're touring – their backstage requirements include eight 'stamped, local postcards'.

- Disney's *The Lion King* has become the most successful re-release ever, after three million copies of the new DVD sold in its first two days on release.

- Rocker Sting is *Titanic* star Leonardo DiCaprio's next-door neighbour in Malibu, California.

——————— ENTERTAINMENT ———————

- Dustin Hoffman had to pass up the chance of appearing in a jury for the first time because he had to publicise his film *Runaway Jury*, in which he plays a lawyer.

- *Friends* star Courtney Cox is scared of dogs – unless they're her own. The actress owns three pooches.

- Pop star Jessica Simpson used to keep photographs of missing children under her pillow and pray for them every night when she was a teenager. She also tried to adopt a Mexican baby found in a dumpster when she was 16.

- Pop couple Jessica Simpson and Nick Lachey have a television mounted in their shower.

- When Orson Welles won the Screenplay Oscar for his classic *Citizen Kane* in 1941, it wasn't a popular choice. The audience booed.

- *American Idol* star Clay Aiken is allergic to mushrooms, shellfish, chocolate, mint and coffee.

- There was havoc on the shoot for Atomic Kitten video 'Ladies Night' – the British trio hired famous drag queen Lily Savage, real name Paul O'Grady, to star, but Savage stormed out when he discovered he was to be appearing alongside a troop of unknown female impersonators.

——————— ENTERTAINMENT ———————

- Gravel-voiced singer Macy Gray has puffer fish pets named Justin Timberlake, Muhammad Ali and R. Kelly.

- Rap mogul Sean 'P Diddy' Combs spends £625 on each of his haircuts. His personal barber sketches out styles before even touching Diddy's dome.

- Bad-boy rapper Eminem's two favourite places to tour are Amsterdam, The Netherlands, because of its liberal laws, and London, England, because of its food.

- Actress Gwyneth Paltrow is studying German, as she endeavours to conquer European languages. She's already fluent in Spanish, Italian and French.

- Super-rich movie beauty Cameron Diaz recently bought a £1.25 Californian lottery ticket – and won £3,125.

- Oscar winner Holly Hunter used to be a poultry judge in her native Georgia.

- *Austin Powers* creator Mike Myers has two streets named after him in his native Toronto, Canada.

- Crooner Harry Connick Jr. quit smoking when his idol Mel Torme told him he'd never speak to him again until he was nicotine free.

ENTERTAINMENT

- At £150 for just two ounces, *Sex and the City*'s Sarah Jessica Parker's SJJL moisturiser contains gold and silver essence.

- Destiny's Child singer Kelly Rowland is so turned off by the cuisine whenever she's in Britain that she will only eat at the country's Caribbean restaurants and posh eatery Nobu.

- *Notting Hill* star Julia Roberts once had her own scent created for the Oscars. It cost £4,000 a litre.

- *Friends* star Jennifer Aniston ate the same lunch – consisting of lettuce, garbanzo beans, turkey and lemon dressing – for nine years.

- Hollywood actor Brad Pitt has topped a survey conducted by American condom makers Trojan as the celebrity women think is most well endowed. Despite his ladykiller reputation, *NSYNC Justin Timberlake didn't make the list's top ten.

- Legendary London nightspot Annabel's welcomed British beauty Elizabeth Hurley on to its management committee in an effort to give the club a sleeker image and encourage younger members to join.

———————— ENTERTAINMENT ————————

- Soul star-turned-Reverend Al Green was so worried about including words like 'baby' and 'sugar' in songs on his album *I Can't Stop* that he asked for guidance from the congregation at his Tennessee church.

- The longest Oscars ceremony, in 2000, lasted a bum-numbing 256 minutes.

- Spanish crooner Julio Iglesias holds the record for selling more albums in more languages than any other singer.

- One Christmas, *Friends* stars Jennifer Aniston, Courtney Cox, Lisa Kudrow, Matt Leblanc, Matthew Perry and David Schwimmer gave plasma TVs to crew members who'd worked on the show for less than five years – while those who'd passed the five-year mark received Mini Cooper cars.

- Rapper Ice Cube's Navigator sports utility vehicle has six television screens in it.

- Before hitting acting success, *Everybody Loves Raymond* star Patricia Heaton worked in New York as a 6am room-service waitress at the Park Le Meridien hotel.

- Hollywood star Tom Cruise had attended 15 schools by the time he was 14.

ENTERTAINMENT

- Alfred Hitchcock directed the first talking film ever made in England. It was called *Blackmail* and was made in 1931.

- *Dynasty* star Joan Collins's late father once served as an agent for *X Factor*'s Sharon Osbourne's dad Don Arden, who was a singer at the time.

- *24* star Kiefer Sutherland has his family's Scottish crest tattooed on his back. It's one of six tattoos the actor boasts.

- Patrick Swayze's first crush was on a dancer his mother taught, called Ellen Smith. The young girl later changed her name to Jaclyn Smyth and became an original *Charlie's Angel*.

- If you decide you don't want your Oscar, you are supposed to sell it back to the academy for $1.

- Late rapper Tupac Shakur – who was shot and killed at the age of 25 in 1996 – came up with his signature shaven hairstyle because he suffered from premature baldness.

- Former Destiny's Child singer Farrah Franklin's middle name is Destiny.

ENTERTAINMENT

- Armourers created 9,000 arrows and 3,000 swords for historical epic *Alexander* starring Colin Farrell.

- The red carpet at the 2004 Grammy Awards turned green because the event was sponsored by beer company Heineken.

- Singer Robbie Williams once posed as a beggar in New York's Times Square and gave £55 to the first person who gave him money.

- The oldest Oscar winner was 81-year-old Jessica Tandy, for *Driving Miss Daisy* in 1989. Gloria Stuart is the oldest nominee ever, nominated in 1997 for *Titanic*. She was 87.

- Singer-turned-children's author Madonna likes to sing 'Truly Scrumptious' from hit musical *Chitty Chitty Bang Bang* to her children Lourdes and Rocco.

- Hollywood star Tom Cruise insists on having his own stuntplane on standby whenever he's on location filming so he can take off and relax high above the earth.

- *Paycheck* star Aaron Eckhart has a pet dog named Dirty.

ENTERTAINMENT

- Wacky screenwriter and director Quentin Tarantino wrote a script called 'Captain Peachfuzz and The Anchovy Bandit' as a child.

- San Francisco-based Neil Diamond tribute group Super Diamond are the world's top covers band – they charge £8,820 per show.

- Destiny's Child star Beyonce Knowles's hit single 'Crazy In Love' was the best-selling mobile-phone ring tone in Britain in 2003.

- Sugar Ray rocker Mark Mcgrath has such an intense fear of elevators that he insists on taking the stairs if he has to travel 40 floors or less.

- Judy Dench clocked up the shortest screen time for an Oscar winner. She won Best Supporting Actress in 1998 for less than eight minutes on screen in *Shakespeare in Love*.

- Hollywood star Bruce Willis holds the record for the biggest payout for voiceover work, after receiving £5.5 million for 1990's *Look Who's Talking Too*.

- Scottish band Texas were named after the 1984 film *Paris, Texas*.

ENTERTAINMENT

- A man in Dallas, Texas, spent his entire life savings – £22,105 – on 6,000 seats for people to see Mel Gibson's movie *The Passion Of The Christ*, because he believes it will 'change' America.

- Mel Gibson and Johnny Depp refused offers by bosses at the 2004 Oscars to present awards because they admitted they'd be far too nervous.

- Rockers U2 use a sound system on tour which weighs 30 tons.

- Hollywood is being hit by a new fad – bio-degradable pants. The two Hobbits Elijah Wood and Sean Astin are fans and hip-hop legend Missy Elliott is meant to be partial to the bizarre bio pants.

- Hit thriller *Jaws 2* was originally going to be called 'More Jaws', but polling showed audiences assumed a film with that name would be a comic spoof.

- There are still two Oscar categories in which no women have ever won – Best Cinematography and the Best Sound.

- *X-Men* actor Hugh Jackman turned down a role in Australian soap opera *Neighbours* at the beginning of his career because he was auditioning for drama schools.

ENTERTAINMENT

- Inspired by Mel Gibson's controversial new movie *The Passion Of The Christ*, replicas of crucifixion nails are selling at select stores around America for £8.94.

- To mark young actor Tyler Hoechlin's 16th birthday, Tom Hanks – who played his father in *Road To Perdition* – sent him $16 (£9).

- The Used singer Bert McCracken has a pet Chihuahua named David Bowie.

- Kate Winslet gave birth to baby son Joe with the music of Rufus Wainwright in the background.

- British heir-to-the-throne Prince Charles has launched his own range of shampoos and conditioners under his company Duchy Originals.

- US Rapper Fat Joe is building a specially designed wardrobe in his new Miami mansion to house his 5,000-plus pairs of running shoes.

- Kathy Richards Hilton, mother of hotel heiress Paris Hilton, went to school with pop singer Janet Jackson.

ENTERTAINMENT

- Potential Oscar winners are told to keep acceptance speeches to 45 seconds – unlike Greer Garson, whose 1942 speech clocked in at seven minutes

- British pop stars Busted helped cure a boy who was told he might never walk again. Seven-year-old Alex Harris had been wheelchair bound with a rare muscle-wasting disease, but tapped his toes after hearing the band for the first time – and now, four months on, he's dancing again.

- Hollywood star Tom Hanks's movies have amassed an impressive total of £2.6 billion since his film career began in 1980.

- The average cost of making a Hollywood movie in 2003 was £57.2 million.

- Hollywood veterans Sophia Loren, Liz Taylor and Raquel Welch were all considered for the role of *Dynasty* TV bitch Alexis before Joan Collins landed the part.

- An English town is to name a street after The Darkness front man Justin Hawkins. The rock star's home of Lowestoft, Suffolk is planning on a Hawkins Way or a Justin Avenue.

ENTERTAINMENT

- Gleneagles Hotel, the original hotel that inspire John Cleese's legendary sitcom *Fawlty Towers*, has been saved from demolition and is being turned into an official tourist landmark in Torquay, Devon, England.

- *Cabaret* star Liza Minnelli is the only Oscar winner with two Oscar-winning parents – her mum, Judy Garland, was a winner in 1939, and her dad, Vincente Minnelli, in 1958.

- Hotel heiress sisters Paris and Nicky Hilton are each expected to inherit £15.5 million when their parents die.

- *Lord of the Rings* director Peter Jackson promised two of his Oscars to his children, because they want to use them as bedside objects.

- Bosses at vacuum cleaner company Dyson have treated *X Factor*'s Sharon Osbourne to a brand new purple hoover, which they've created to pick up animal hair and excrement.

- US comedienne Ellen Degeneres and singer Harry Connick Jr.'s fathers worked on a paper round together as children in their native New Orleans, Louisiana.

ENTERTAINMENT

- Three generations of the Astin family have acted in director Peter Jackson's films. Sean Astin played Samwise Gamgee in *The Lord Of The Rings* trilogy; his young daughter Ali played his child in *The Return Of The King*, and his dad John Astin appeared in Jackson's 1996 movie *The Frighteners*.

- Action hero Harrison Ford is so in love with fiancée Calista Flockhart that he drinks out of a cup decorated with their pictures and names.

- Patrick Presley, 31, a cousin of rock legend Elvis, hanged himself while in jail in Mississippi over a fatal car accident.

- US singer Justin Timberlake's 2003 Christmas show in Dublin, Ireland, sold out in 40 seconds.

- Around 5,800 people on the Academy of Motion Picture Arts and Sciences' panel vote for the Oscars.

- Terrorist group leader Osama Bin Ladin's niece Waffa is considering changing her name to Deborah before launching a pop career in America. Waffa has been working on material with Madonna producer Nellee Hooper and John Benson, the man who discovered All Saints.

--- **ENTERTAINMENT** ---

- *Playboy* magnate Hugh Hefner auctioned off his address book containing the phone numbers of some of the most beautiful women in the world – along with memorabilia including portraits of Marilyn Monroe, Madonna and Brigitte Bardot – to mark the 50th anniversary of the men's magazine.

- Justin Timberlake was so impressed by Queen's 'Bohemian Rhapsody' as a child that he locked himself away in his bedroom for two days straight to listen to the track over and over again.

- *Bridget Jones* star Renee Zellweger carries two mobile phones around with her – one for calls from England and the other for American calls.

- US talk-show legend Oprah Winfrey sleeps on Frette bed sheets, which boast a very high thread count and sell for up to £1,500 a set.

- Troubled singer Michael Jackson once paid £14,705 to hire two private jets – one for him to travel in and another as a decoy to confuse the press when he travelled from Las Vegas, Nevada, to Santa Barbara, California.

- Funnyman Mike Myers's wedding ring is his late father's 1956 *Encyclopaedia Britannica* Salesman of The Year gift.

—————— ENTERTAINMENT ——————

- Singer-turned-actress Cher refuses to watch hit movie *Thelma & Louise* – she turned down Geena Davis's role.

- The original title of cult TV show *Charlie's Angels* was Alleycats.

- *Catwoman* star Halle Berry's stint on American satire show *Saturday Night Live* was so chaotic that she appeared for the final curtain call with her boots on the wrong feet.

- Supermodel Claudia Schiffer was paid an incredible £200,000 to make a one-minute cameo in Hugh Grant's film *Love Actually*.

- Accident-prone *Lord Of The Rings* star Orlando Bloom has broken his skull three times, both legs, a finger, a toe, a rib, an arm, a wrist, his nose and his back.

- US movie star Billy Bob Thornton once spent 18 months working in a Los Angeles pizza parlour. He was so good he worked his way up to assistant manager.

- The gun that killed outlaw Jesse James sold at auction in Anaheim, California, for £218,750 on 10 November 2003. The winning bid is a new record for a Western history firearm.

ENTERTAINMENT

- The first thing *King Arthur* star Keira Knightley bought with her first movie paycheque was a doll's house.

- US rocker Pink has a ritual every time she releases a new album – she takes a bottle of champagne to New York's Virgin Megastore and buys the first copy.

- Singer Madonna once worked as a coat-check girl at New York's Russian Tea Room restaurant, but she was fired for wearing fishnet stockings.

- Hollywood star Denzel Washington and his wife Pauletta have a special trophy room in their California home to display all of their accolades. While Washington has won awards – including two Academy Awards – for his acting, his spouse has been honoured many times over as a concert pianist.

- US singer and actress Jennifer Lopez stores her lavish pink diamond engagement ring in a safe when she's filming.

- Duran Duran frontman Simon Le Bon has historical controversy in his past – he can trace his family tree back to Europe's Huguenots who were forced to find refuge in England after being chased out of France by the Catholics for their Protestant beliefs.

———————— ENTERTAINMENT ————————

- Teenage rap sensation Bow Wow's monthly allowance is £3,750.

- Roc-A-Fella hip-hop mogul Damon Dash – who owns more than 3,000 pairs of trainers – never wears the same clothes twice, and refuses to write in red ink because it signifies losing money.

- *Charlie's Angels* star Cameron Diaz insists on being environmentally friendly even when she's being ferried to awards shows and events – she uses Los Angeles' Evo Limo Luxury Car Service, where all vehicles run on natural gases.

- US actress Brooke Shields can trace her heritage back to King Henry IV of France and Lucrezia Borgia.

- Legendary rocker Ozzy Osbourne and opera singer Sarah Brightman used to go to the same vocal coach in London.

- US diva Barbra Streisand insisted on spraying her black microphone white for her performance on the *Oprah Winfrey Show* so it matched her off-white outfit.

- Magician David Blaine opted to fast in a box above London's River Thames for 44 days because the number correlates with his birthday, 4 April.

ENTERTAINMENT

- US rapper Lil Kim's manicurist charges up to £3,125 a day to wrap her nails in shredded $100 bills.

- Two of US actor Ashton Kutcher's toes on his right foot are stuck together.

- America's first reality-TV awards were scrapped because network bosses refused to offer clips to the organisers. Producer Don Mischer has cited lack of network co-operation for his decision to cancel the first Reality Awards.

- Rock matriarch Sharon Osbourne keeps her hands soft with peanut oil – the same concoction she uses to stop the wooden counter tops in her kitchen from drying out.

- Hollywood legend Zsa Zsa Gabor hosted the Rubik's cube's launch in America, beginning with a Hollywood party on 5 May 1980.

- US President Gerald Ford once worked as a cover model for *Cosmopolitan* magazine.

- When the decision was made in 1962 that cartoon family the Flintstones would have a baby, the child was going to be a boy. Later, they decided that a girl would make for better merchandising like dolls, etc.

ENTERTAINMENT

- US rapper Sean 'P Diddy' Combs is such a fan of Al Pacino's *Scarface* movie that he has watched it 63 times.

- Former TV *Superman* Dean Cain was a onetime football star in Buffalo, New York. The actor signed for the Buffalo Bills after leaving Princeton University but seriously injured his knee and had to retire before he had played a game for the team.

- Pop diva Jennifer Lopez demanded her on-set trailer on *Shall We Dance?* be stocked with diet cream soda, despite the fact that the drink is unavailable to buy where the movie is being shot in Winnipeg, Canada. Supplies had to be flown in from Seattle, America.

- An alternative title for sitcom *Friends* was Insomnia Cafe.

- American funnyman Jerry Seinfeld received £315,000 for a 15-minute gig in Las Vegas.

- *The Wedding Singer* star Adam Sandler is currently the world's highest-paid actor, according to the new *Guinness World Records* list. Sandler, 36, is said to have taken home a massive £31 million in 2001.

ENTERTAINMENT

- While attending America's University of Iowa, actor Ashton Kutcher helped pay his tuition fees by sweeping floors at a local General Mills plant.

- Between takes on movie *Shall We Dance?*, Jennifer Lopez ate strawberry muffins and ice cream 'almost every day'.

- US singer and actress Hilary Duff is set to launch a new line of canine clothing called Little Dog Duff, named after her own pooch Little Dog.

- Hard rocker Andrew WK has named his new album after his most loyal fans. The Party Hard star has named his album *Wolf* after the W.K. Wolves who follow him on tour.

- Australian pop beauty Holly Valance's real surname is Vuckadinovic.

- *Alexander* star Colin Farrell often checks into hotels under the name Tom Foolery, while *American Pie* actress Tara Reid regularly adopts the moniker Strawberry Shortcake. *The Truth About Love* star Jennifer Love Hewitt dubs herself Winnie The Pooh.

ENTERTAINMENT

- *The Osbournes* star Jack Osbourne has had 'Mum' tattooed in a heart on his left shoulder as a special thank you to mum Sharon, who helped him battle his drug- and alcohol-abuse problems.

- *American Idol* bosses have banned wannabe pop stars from singing Alicia Keys's 'Fallin'' in try-outs, because judges Simon Cowell, Randy Jackson and Paula Abdul are tired of the song.

- *Baywatch*'s Pamela Anderson failed her first driving test when she hit another car. She passed at the fourth attempt.

- Hollywood heartthrob George Clooney bought a couple of *Charlie's Angels* star Lucy Liu's arty collages when she had a brief stint with him on *ER*.

- Pop babe Beyonce Knowles spends £4,000 a week on personal trainer Mark Jenkins in order to maintain her stunning physique.

- Rap mogul Russell Simmons and his wife have different refrigerators because the DEF JAM founder doesn't want his vegan food mixed with her chicken, fish and dairy products.

ENTERTAINMENT

- Veteran rocker Bruce Springsteen's triumphant concert at Boston's Fenway Park on 6 September 2003 was the first rock show in the baseball stadium's 91-year history.

- Comedienne Ellen Degeneres has had a ping-pong table installed on the set of her new chat show *The Ellen Degeneres Show* to encourage her colleagues to play as hard as they work.

- British singer Robbie Williams refuses to let his lack of a driving licence stop him splashing out on cars. The Los Angeles-based star, who has never passed a driving test, already has a Ferrari and a Jaguar – and now he's looking at a £200,000 Lamborghini Diablo.

- Rappers 50 Cent and Eminem had very simple backstage requests at the MTV Music Video Awards; while other stars were demanding bowls of raw vegetables and expensive alcohol, the rap pair asked for four boxes of Kentucky Fried Chicken and large portions of Mexican treats from Taco Bell.

- British women have voted former Spice Girls singer Victoria Beckham as the most boring celebrity to socialise with.

ENTERTAINMENT

- Wild-living rocker Ozzy Osbourne has installed a 12-metre (20ft) water jet at his Los Angeles home, which will soak anyone who comes near the house without an invitation in order to deter potential thieves.

- With an empire consisting of Bad Boy Entertainment, Sean John clothing, Blue Flame marketing and advertising, Justin's restaurants and MTV show Making The Band 2, rap mogul Sean 'P Diddy' Combs, 32, has been ranked 12th in *Fortune* magazine's Under-40 list, which ranks those under the age of 40 who've become multimillionaires.

- Celebrity parents Will Smith, Madonna, Chris O'Donnell and Kevin Kline are among the many stars who have splashed out on Posh Tots' mini mansions, castles and chalets for their children to play in. The prices for the little homes range from £29,375 to £54,693.

- The Karl Lagerfeld-designed Chanel dress that *Sex in the City*'s Sarah Jessica Parker wore to the 2003 Emmy Awards took 250 hours to make.

- US talk-show host Oprah Winfrey says her two favourite interviews of all time were with Sidney Poitier and Salma Hayek.

———————— ENTERTAINMENT ————————

● Athens-born rocker Tommy Lee's mother was Miss Greece in 1957.

● Actress Daryl Hannah's brother Don is a skydiving instructor.

● Rocker Simon Le Bon often checks into hotels under the name Shake Yabooty, while rapper Wyclef Jean calls himself Dracula and US singer Brian McKnight opts for Albert Einstein.

● Michael Caine's movie *Secondhand Lions* was made after the filmscript topped a magazine list of the 10 best scripts never made into a film.

● US actress Drew Barrymore mixed together cream of mushroom soup and stuffing to make her vomit look authentic on the set of comedy *Duplex*.

● Hollywood star Ben Affleck appeared as an extra – playing a basketball player – in the 1992 surprise hit film *Buffy the Vampire Slayer*.

● Czech supermodel Karolina Kurkova's father doubled up as a police chief and a basketball professional when she was a child growing up in Decin.

ENTERTAINMENT

- Rapper NAS's 30th birthday cake was iced with green marijuana leaves, as a nod to his hemp advocacy.

- Presenters and nominees at the 2003 Emmy Awards received a gift basket worth more than £18,750 featuring speciality phones and a trip to Bora Bora.

- US actress Rena Sofer, who stars in the American version of saucy British sitcom *Coupling*, is an orthodox rabbi.

- Legendary singer Sir Elton John refuses to play white pianos which he brands 'tasteless'. He also dislikes white limousines, but he can tolerate one item in white – refrigerators.

- US rappers Eminem and Wyclef Jean were born on the same day in the same year, 17 October 1972.

- Rocker Dave Matthews and his wife Ashley have matching wedding bands made out of pressed pennies from the years they were born, 1967 and 1973.

- Flamboyant comic Eddie Izzard managed to practically sell out his Sexie show at New York's City Centre despite having virtually no advertising or promotion.

ENTERTAINMENT

- Director Quentin Tarantino was so impressed with the bar from the fictitious House of Blue Leaves, created for his movie *Kill Bill*, he had it installed in his Hollywood home.

- Funnyman Jim Carrey, comedienne Ellen Degeneres and *Frasier* star Jane Leeves were in the same acting class before hitting fame.

- Actress Uma Thurman carried home rocks from the different locations where she filmed *Kill Bill* for her children Maya, five, and Roan, one.

- *Everybody Loves Raymond* star Ray Romano went to high school with actress Fran Drescher in New York, and refused to be funny in her presence because he couldn't stand her nasal laugh.

- Radiohead star Jonny Greenwood has turned composer – he has penned the score for new human life on earth TV documentary *Bodysong*.

- Rapper 50 Cent's new £2.6 million mansion in Farmington, Connecticut, is the largest in the entire state. The pad used to belong to Mike Tyson and boasts 18 bedrooms, 38 bathrooms and a manmade waterfall.

ENTERTAINMENT

- Dublin kebab restaurant Abrakebabra rewarded heavyweight Westlife singer Bryan McFadden with a gold card to thank him for being their best customer.

- Rapper Eminem's parents once fronted a covers group called Daddy Warbucks.

- Movie funnyman Bill Murray owns a little-league baseball team in St Paul, Minnesota, and helps boost attendances by inviting fans to try out the hot tub he has installed in the stand.

- Football-mad rocker Rod Stewart's nine-year-old son with model Rachel Hunter, Liam McAllister Stewart, is named after Scottish international sport hero Gary McAllister.

- Friends star Jennifer Aniston wore underwear with a picture of Brad Pitt on it to the 2003 Emmy Awards.

- Welsh actress Catherine Zeta Jones's son Dylan has become so close to his mother's pal George Clooney that he now refers to the actor as Uncle George.

ENTERTAINMENT

- Reportedly flamboyant rocker Sir Elton John is having a range of candles made for him with specially designed wicks, as he can't sleep unless he has personally trimmed them before going to bed.

- Staff at supermarket Tesco's were so impressed with a special extra-large species of South African avocado that they've christened it the J.Lo after Jennifer Lopez's impressive curves.

- US actor Kevin Costner has twice taken on roles after Harrison Ford turned them down – Ford was the original choice to star in *Dragonfly* and *JFK*.

- The name of 4-LOM, one the bounty hunters listening to Darth Vader in *The Empire Strikes Back*, means: For Love Of Money.

- Hollywood funnyman Jim Carrey voted in 2004 at the Beverly Hills City Hall. He had an assistant wait in line for him, however.

- Police in Italy had to come to UK supermodel Naomi Campbell's rescue when a crowd of up to 4,000 men swarmed a beach.

ENTERTAINMENT

- The Russian Imperial Necklace has been loaned out by Joseff jewellers of Hollywood for 1,215 different feature films.

- *Titanic* star Leonardo DiCaprio says he practised his losing smile for the Oscars – because he knew he wouldn't win the Best Actor trophy.

- There is a new television show on a British cable channel called *Watching Paint Dry*. Viewers watch in real-time: gloss, semi-gloss, matt, satin, you name it. Then viewers vote out their least favourite.

- The BBC asked to interview reggae legend Bob Marley for a documentary – despite the fact he died in 1981. They sent the Bob Marley Foundation an email saying it would involve him 'spending one or two days with us'.

- Thousands of Britons say they would like Robbie Williams's song 'Angels' played at their funeral.

- In *Star Wars*, a small pair of metal dice can be seen hanging in the Millennium Falcon's cockpit as Chewbacca prepares to depart from Mos Eisley. The dice do not appear in subsequent scenes.

ENTERTAINMENT

- Zeppo Marx (the unfunny one of the Marx Brothers) had a patent for a wristwatch with a heart monitor.

- A schoolgirl asked band Coldplay for their autographs to sell for charity – and got a triple platinum disc worth £4,000.

- Flamenco dancer Jose Greco took out an insurance policy through Lloyd's of London against his pants splitting during a performance.

- Jonathan Davids, lead singer of Korn, played in his high-school bagpipe band.

- Rap artist Sean 'P Diddy' Combs had his first job aged two when he modelled in an ad for Baskin-Robbins ice-cream shops.

- *ET* director Steven Spielberg is Drew Barrymore's god-father. After seeing her nude in *Playboy* magazine, he sent her a blanket with a note telling her to cover herself up.

- In 1996, 37% of the toys sold in the United States were Star Wars products.

- *Speed* star Sandra Bullock has revealed she uses haemorrhoid cream on her face.

ENTERTAINMENT

- The Monty Python movie *The Life of Brian* was banned in Scotland on its release.

- In 1977, the legendary Groucho Marx died three days after Elvis Presley died. Unfortunately, due to the fevered commotion caused by Presley's unanticipated death, the media paid little attention to the passing of this brilliant comic.

- *Men in Black* star Will Smith wants female fans to stop asking him to sign their breasts – because he doesn't want to upset their boyfriends.

- Actor Robert De Niro played the part of the Cowardly Lion in his elementary school's production of *The Wizard of Oz*. De Niro was ten at the time.

- Rudolph the Red-Nosed Reindeer was created in 1939, in Chicago, for the Montgomery Ward department stores for a Christmas promotion. The lyrics were written as a poem 'Rollo, the red-nosed reindeer' by Robert May. Montgomery Ward in Chicago liked it but didn't like the name Rollo so they changed it to Rudolph. It wasn't set to music until 1947 and Gene Autry recorded the hit song in 1949.

─────── ENTERTAINMENT ───────

- The first Michelin Man costume (Bidenbum) was worn by none other than Col. Harlan Sanders of Kentucky Fried Chicken fame.

- Former *EastEnders* star Danniella Westbrook buys her millionaire husband clothes on eBay.

- In Estonia, *Teletubbies* is known as *teletupsuds*.

- Winnie the Pooh author AA Milne's name is Alan Alexander Milne.

- *Teletubbies* is filmed in the open on a site in Warwickshire. The dome, hills and rabbits are real. Some of the grass and flowers are real and some are artificial.

- You cannot walk down the Disney parade route without being on at least one camera.

- In *Star Wars*, actress Jodie Foster was George Lucas's second choice to play the part of Princess Leia.

- In 1978, the Hollywood sign was in such a state of disrepair (termites had infested the wooden scaffolding that supports the 15m-high letters) that one of the Os had fallen off.

ENTERTAINMENT

- After 50 events, the UK claims to be the most successful Eurovision nation – Ireland have won more often with seven victories to the UK's five but the UK have finished 2nd an astonishing 15 times.

- A shocking *EastEnders* storyline featuring Dennis Rickman having an affair with Peggy Mitchell was pulled at the last minute.

- Ex-Van Halen frontman David Lee Roth cancelled the rest of his US tour after injuring himself performing 'a very fast, complicated 15th-century samurai move' during a recent performance.

- In 2004, Rocker David Bowie thought he was being stalked by someone dressed as a giant pink rabbit. Bowie has noticed the fan at several recent concerts, but he became alarmed when he got on a plane and the bunny was on board.

- The beginning of *The Wizard of Oz* is black and white because colour was not available at that point. When colour was available, the writers decided to start using it in Munchkinland.

ENTERTAINMENT

- Television presenter Johnny Vaughan says his £60,000 sports car was crashed by his pet bulldog Harvey. Vaughan had stopped his automatic Maserati 3200GT on the way home from a visit to a vet, thinking Harvey needed the toilet, but, when he got out of the vehicle, Harvey jumped across the seat and hit the gear stick into drive.

- Stars received an unusual gift in their goodie bag at this year's Oscars – a vacuum cleaner.

- Hal in *2001: Space Odyssey* got his name from the producers of the film. HAL are the letters before IBM (H comes before I, A before B and L before M)

- Napoleon Bonaparte is the historical figure most often portrayed in movies. He has been featured in 194 movies, Jesus Christ in 152 and Abraham Lincoln in 137.

- While on a training schedule and drinking protein drinks to enhance her muscles, Hollywood superstar Halle Berry confessed she couldn't stop breaking wind as a result of the drinks.

- Chewbacca's name is inspired by the name of Chebika City, in Tunisia, near the place where Tatooine scenes in *Star Wars* where shot.

------------------ **ENTERTAINMENT** ------------------

- Nicole Richie has six pet rats and gave her *Simple Life* co-star Paris Hilton a rat she called 'Tori Spelling' for Christmas.

- Glamour model Jordan once said she fancied a six-in-a-bed romp with five other celebrities – but not the Beckhams.

- In 1965, auditions were held for the *Monkees* TV show. Some of the people who responded (but were not hired) were Stephen Stills, Harry Nilsson, and Paul Williams.

- *American Beauty* star Kevin Spacey's older brother is a professional Rod Stewart impersonator.

- A BBC children's presenter was reprimanded for wearing a T-shirt that contained a risqué slogan. Dominic Wood was rapped for wearing a 'Morning Wood' T-shirt on his *Dick and Dom in da Bungalow* show.

- Irish singer Ronan Keating had to abandon a filming session when he was flashed at by streakers in Phuket.

- A mouse caused £7,000 damage to BBC television presenter Sue Barker's Ferrari.

ENTERTAINMENT

- David Letterman was voted Class Smart Alec at his home town high school, Broad Ripple High.

- La Boca in Southern Buenos Aires, Argentina, is the birthplace of the tango.

- *Basic Instinct* star Sharon Stone is a member of MENSA.

- The Millennium Falcon in *Star Wars* was originally inspired by the shape of a hamburger with an olive on the side.

- Singer Lenny Kravitz kept a marijuana joint he'd shared with Rolling Stone Mick Jagger for a year as a tribute.

- In *The Empire Strikes Back*, legendary actor Alec Guinness performed all his appearances in six hours.

- The Swedish pop group ABBA recently turned down an offer of £1 billion to reunite.

- In 1962, the Mashed Potato, the Loco-Motion, the Frug, the Monkey and the Funky Chicken were popular dances.

- *Friends* star Lisa Kudrow has a degree in biology from Vassar College.

ENTERTAINMENT

- Hollywood legend Paul Newman is colour-blind.

- *Miss Congeniality* star Sandra Bullock is allergic to horses.

- US actress Lara Flynn Boyle is dyslexic.

- *9½ Weeks* star Kim Basinger has suffered panic attacks during which she cannot leave the house.

- *Austin Powers* star Mike Myers has an aversion to being touched.

- *Charlie and the Chocolate Factory* star Johnny Depp is afraid of clowns.

- *Four Weddings and a Funeral actress* Andie MacDowell worked at McDonald's and Pizza Hut as a teen.

- US funnyman Steve Martin once worked at Disneyland selling maps and guidebooks.

- *Matrix* star Keanu Reeves father has served time in prison for cocaine possession.

- *Cheers* actor Woody Harrelson's father has served time in prison for murder.

ENTERTAINMENT

- *Red Dragon* actor Edward Norton's father invented the shopping mall.

- *ER* actress Julianna Margulies's father wrote the 'Plop-Plop, Fizz-Fizz' Alka-Seltzer commercial.

- *Baywatch*'s David Hasselhoff's great-uncle was Karl Hasselhoff, the inventor of inflatable sheep.

- Singer Eric Clapton owns one-fifth of the planet Mars.

- In the film *Forrest Gump*, all the still photos show Forrest with his eyes closed.

- Toto the dog was paid £65 per week while filming *The Wizard of Oz*.

- Kelsey Grammar sings and plays the piano for the theme song of *Frasier*.

- The director of *Charlie and the Chocolate Factory*, Tim Burton, spent millions on training squirrels to crack nuts to recreate the 'Nut Room' scene.

- Cinderella's slippers were originally made out of fur. The story was changed in the 1600s by a translator.

—————————— ENTERTAINMENT ——————————

- Pupils at a US school have been offered counselling after a teacher showed them clips of Mel Gibson's film *The Passion of the Christ*.

- *Pop Idol* runner-up Gareth Gates fan missed meeting him when he turned up at her home because her dad had the television on too loud.

- An elderly actor who broke his leg on stage during a performance of Nobel Prize winner Dario Fo's *The Accidental Death of an Anarchist* in Bosnia had to endure laughs and taunts from the audience who thought his cries of pain were part of the show.

- Pinocchio was made of pine.

- In the opening scene of *Raiders of the Lost Ark*, Indy escapes with the golden idol in a seaplane with the registration number OB-3PO. This, of course refers to Obi-wan and C-3PO from *Star Wars*.

- The 'Mexican Hat Dance' is the official dance of Mexico.

- Professional ballerinas use about 12 pairs of toe shoes per week.

ENTERTAINMENT

- US singer Macy Gray stunned fans by performing naked on stage – apart from a pair of designer shoes.

- For *Star Wars'* 20th anniversary, the first episode film renovation cost as much as the original movie.

- Former Generation-X singer Billy Idol has revealed he shaves his grey pubic hair.

- Over eight years of *Seinfeld*, 'Cosmo' Kramer went through Jerry Seinfeld's apartment door 284 times.

- Actress Elizabeth Hurley has 12 piercings in her ears and a pierced nose.

- Buskers in Budapest are to have to take a yearly exam to protect tourists from musically incompetent beggars.

- A rock fan who paid £1,000 for a guitar signed by Queen's Brian May rubbed off the signature with his sleeve when he played it.

- In all three *Godfather* films, when you see oranges, there is a death (or a very close call) coming up soon.

- Prince Charles sent a bottle of whisky to recovering alcoholic Ozzy Osbourne after his quad bike crash.

ENTERTAINMENT

- When director George Lucas was mixing the *American Graffiti* soundtrack, he numbered the reels of film starting with an 'R' and numbered the dialogue starting with a 'D'. Sound designer Walter Murch asked George for Reel 2, Dialogue 2 by saying 'R2D2'. George liked the way that sounded so much he integrated that into another project he was working on.

- Singer Janet Jackson's boob flash at the Super Bowl has become the most searched event in the history of the internet.

- It was the left shoe that Cinderella lost at the stairway, when the prince tried to follow her.

- It was illegal to sell ET dolls in France because there is a law against selling dolls without human faces.

- DJ Jo Whiley has gone under the knife to have a third nipple removed. She had thought it was a mole until doctors informed her otherwise.

- The Paramount logo contains 22 stars.

- Donald Duck lives at 1313 Webfoot Walk, Duckburg, Calisota.

— ENTERTAINMENT —

- The small actor hiding inside R2-D2 is named Kenny Baker and is less than 4 feet tall

- Canadian singer Bryan Adams's song 'Everything I Do (I Do It For You)' is the track most couples pick for the first dance at their weddings.

- By the time a child finishes primary school he will have witnessed 8,000 murders and 100,000 acts of violence on television.

- Veteran crooner Tony Christie has landed a £50,000 contract to become the face of Stilton cheese.

- Sections of the under-construction Death Star in *Star Wars* resemble the San Francisco skyline, the silhouette of a favourite city of George Lucas.

- The Smiths have been studied at an academic conference in their home town of Manchester.

- In 1912, the Archbishop of Paris declared dancing the tango a sin.

- One of the many Tarzans, Karmuela Searlel, was mauled to death on the set by a raging elephant.

ENTERTAINMENT

- The most popular TV show in Venezuela is the *Miss Venezuela Pageant*.

- A man who lost £20,000 worth of prizes on ITV1's *Ant and Dec's Saturday Night Takeaway* crashed his car after leaving the studio.

- *Return of the Jedi* was originally titled 'Revenge of the Jedi' – but later underwent a title change, because, according to director George Lucas, a Jedi would never take revenge.

- Television presenter Nick Owen was turned away from a football club bar which is named after him. The BBC *Midlands Today* presenter was trying to get into the Nick Owen bar at Luton Town Football Club but was refused entry because the bar was full.

- Scenes showing Irish actor Colin Farrell's penis have been cut from a new film he's made – because it's too distracting for audiences.

- Jackie Stallone, mother of *Rocky* star Sylvester, says she believes her dogs possess psychic powers because they predicted George Bush would win the US election.

BUSINESS AND COMMERCE

––––––––– **BUSINESS AND COMMERCE** –––––––––

- One of the richest self-made Americans under 40 is Michael Dell, chairman of Dell Computers. He is worth $18 billion.

- There are an average of 18,000,000 items for sale at any time on eBay.

- On eBay, there are an average of $680 worth of transactions each second.

- One in ten Europeans was conceived on an Ikea bed, say the company.

- The red spot on the 7up cans comes from its inventor, who was an albino.

- Researchers believe businessmen could be increasing their risk of eye disease by wearing their ties too tight.

- American office workers send an average of 36 emails per day.

- Fifty-three per cent of Americans think they are paid the right amount.

- Twelve per cent of US businessmen wear their ties so tight that they restrict the blood flow to their brain.

—————— **BUSINESS AND COMMERCE** ——————

- Dismal first-year sales of famous products: VW Beetle (US) 330; Liquid Paper (Tippex) 1,200 bottles; Cuisinart 200; Remington typewriter eight; Scrabble 532; Coca-Cola 25 bottles.

- Dr George F Grant received US patent number 638,920 on 12 December 1899 for his invention – the golf tee. He created it because he didn't want to get his hands dirty by building a mound of dirt to place his ball on.

- One in six employees say they got so mad at a co-worker last year that 'they felt like hitting them but didn't'.

- Dr Guillotin merely proposed the machine that bears his name (which was rejected by the Crown) and he never made a working model. The first working model was made by his assistant years later. When the machine attained infamy in the French Revolution, Dr Guillotin protested its use and went to his grave claiming that the machine was unjustly named after him.

- Draftsmen have to make 27,000 drawings for the manufacturing of a new car.

- At General Motors, the cost of health care for employees now exceeds the cost of steel.

BUSINESS AND COMMERCE

- According to market research firm NPD Fashionworld, 50% of all lingerie purchases are returned to the store.

- A Bedfordshire man was sent a letter from Prudential insurance company addressed to Mr A Shagslikeadonkey.

- Twenty-three per cent of workers said they would work harder if their employer offered a '£500 shopping spree at a store of their choice'.

- A Colombian airline has promised free flights for life to a baby born on board one of their planes.

- Were the Smarties brand to be sold, its value is estimated at £73 million – up £15 million in the last four years following the introduction of spin-off products including the Smarties bar.

- More copies of the Ikea catalogue are printed each year than the Bible.

- Eleven top executives of the US Direct Marketing Association (the telemarketers' group that is trying to kill the federal 'Do Not Call' list) have registered for the list themselves.

———— BUSINESS AND COMMERCE ————

- A Sao Paulo shopping mall is offering five minutes in an oxygen mask to any customer who spends more than the equivalent of £6.

- A woman who went shopping at an Asda store in the West Midlands once found £15,000 in cash on the floor near a checkout.

- One in seven workers needs help turning their office computers on or off because of their dismal knowledge of new technology.

- A Berkshire man once sold a piece of toast on eBay which he says has the face of Joe Pasquale.

- Grocery shoppers spend an average of eight minutes waiting in line at the supermarket.

- A courier firm in Germany is on the verge of bankruptcy after an employee ran up a £20,000 mobile phone bill by calling sex hotlines.

- A Sydney man has pocketed £415 after auctioning a piece of breakfast cereal resembling ET.

───────── **BUSINESS AND COMMERCE** ─────────

● Researchers have found Britons spend more than three
  ✓ hours of every working day gossiping, emailing friends
  and flirting.

● The drink Gatorade was named after the University of
  Florida Gators where it was first developed.

● Proctor & Gamble originally manufactured candles
  before moving on to soap.

● British people have longer relationships with some of
  their household appliances than with their partners.

● A US woman has sold a ten-year-old sandwich said to
  feature the face of the Virgin Mary for £15,000.

● A West Midlands coach company is giving older
  passengers a herbal spray to stop them snoring on long
  journeys.

● There are 1,008 McDonald's franchises in France.

● Blue neckties sell best, followed by red ones.

● The average car in Japan is driven 4,400 miles per year,
  in the US it is 9,500 miles per year.

BUSINESS AND COMMERCE

- Belgians have tried to deliver mail using cats. It didn't work.

- A man once received a bill from British Gas for £2.3 trillion after a computer mix-up.

- A massive 20.5 billion text messages were sent in the UK in 2003.

- A man believed to be the US's oldest worker has retired at the age of 104.

- Viagra became the top-selling medicine in Venezuela during the country's two-month general strike.

- Five years ago, 60% of all retail purchases were made with cash or cheque. Now it's 50%. By 2010, 39% of purchases will be made by cash or cheque.

- The world's first bra made completely of chocolate has gone on sale in Austria.

- One of Britain's largest exam boards is introducing a vocational qualification in wheel clamping.

- Ancient Rome had a rent-a-chariot business.

─────── BUSINESS AND COMMERCE ───────

- German tram passengers are having their stops announced by the voice of Gerhard Schroeder.

- Forty per cent of McDonald's profits comes from the sale of Happy Meals.

- Jeans made from stinging nettles have gone on sale in the UK.

- An Indian council is dumping rubbish outside businesses who don't pay their taxes to try to get them to pay up.

- A restaurant in west London is offering an ashtray amnesty to mark its 10th birthday.

- Great Britain has the highest European consumption of ice cream.

- The first Christmas card was printed in the US in 1875 by Louis Prang, a Massachusetts printer.

- A Berlin man is carving out a new business selling engraved toothpicks.

- George Eastman, inventor of the Kodak camera, hated having his picture taken.

————— **BUSINESS AND COMMERCE** —————

- The first postage stamp to commemorate Christmas was printed in 1937 in Austria.

- In 1810, Peter Durand invented the tin can for preserving food.

- A German firm is printing novels on rolls of toilet paper to 'kill two birds with one stone'.

- There is a Starbucks in Myungdong, South Korea that is five storeys tall.

- The first in-flight movie was shown on 6 April 1925; it was a silent film on a Deutsche Lufthansa flight.

- The Chinese airline Sichuan Airlines has paid £170,000 for the phone number 8888-8888, saying it hopes to make its customers happy, eight being a lucky number in China.

- More than two-thirds of Britain's workers never take the daily breaks they are entitled to because they are too busy.

- A survey has concluded Tesco has the easiest shopping trolleys to control.

———— BUSINESS AND COMMERCE ————

- There has been no mail delivery in Canada on Saturday for the last 35 years.

- A German filling station is employing topless assistants in an attempt to boost trade.

- A Scottish employment quango is under fire after getting its staff to wear T-shirts saying 'Make it in Scotland' that were actually made in Morocco.

- A museum dedicated to traffic signs has opened in the Brazilian city of Sao Paulo.

- A lingerie designer has created a matching bra and knickers out of human hair and is selling them for £2,000 a set.

- The Malaysian government has banned car adverts featuring Brad Pitt because they are 'an insult to Asians'.

- In 1993, the board of governors at Carl Karcher Enterprises voted (5 to 2) to fire Carl Karcher. Carl Karcher is the founder of Carls Jr. restaurants.

- A Swedish man was awarded nearly £60,000 compensation after he was sacked for telling off a colleague for breaking wind.

BUSINESS AND COMMERCE

- Heidi Klum, once voted Germany's most erotic woman, has launched her own collection of orthopaedic sandals.

- David McConnell started the California Perfume Company (CPC) in 1886. Today the company is known as Avon, which he named after his favourite playwright William Shakespeare and Stratford upon Avon.

- Pampers disposable nappies were invented in 1961.

- A Leicestershire firm has been forced to stop giving workers free Christmas turkeys after a ruling by the Inland Revenue.

- A Norwich sex shop had to change an advertisement after council officials objected to the use of the word 'gadget'.

- A shop has opened in London which only sells tomato ketchup.

- Delia Smith once admitted she didn't always cook everything when she used to make tea for her husband's cricket club.

- The Starbucks at the highest elevation is on Main Street in Breckenridge, Colorado.

---------- **BUSINESS AND COMMERCE** ----------

- The US Postal Service owns 176,000 cars and trucks, the largest civilian vehicle fleet on earth.

- When Coca-Cola began to be sold in China, they used characters that would sound like 'Coca-Cola' when spoken. Unfortunately, what it ended up meaning was 'Bite the wax tadpole'. It did not sell well.

- A school has been set up in Italy to teach people how to become drag queens.

- Energy giant Powergen says it has no connection to the unfortunately named Italian website www.powergenitalia.com.

- An outdoor clothing company is changing its name for the Australian market because men don't want the name 'fairy' on their clothing.

- A man who began working for a Ford dealership in West Yorkshire in 1930 was still working at the age of 92.

- A supermarket in Brazil is attracting shoppers by giving them the chance to win a job.

- A scud missile complete with its own launcher truck has been up for sale on eBay.

———— BUSINESS AND COMMERCE ————

- A shopping centre dedicated to the gay community has opened in Brazil.

- A music channel advertised on cows at the Glastonbury Festival.

- Sainsbury's has introduced purple carrots into its range of vegetables.

- A New Zealand town once produced its own postage stamp, but put the sticky bit on the wrong side.

- The working wives of most married millionaires tend to be teachers.

- In 2004, Virgin Atlantic Airlines introduced a double bed for first-class passengers who fly together.

- A Chinese department store has opened a husbands' centre for men who don't want to go shopping with their wives.

- German brothels are to be ordered to offer work experience and trainee posts if they want to continue doing business.

――――――― **BUSINESS AND COMMERCE** ―――――――

- *Sports Illustrated* magazine allows subscribers to opt out of receiving the famous swimsuit issue each year. Fewer than 1% of subscribers choose this option.

- Workers make 15,000 calls to sex and chat lines every hour, costing UK business millions of pounds a year, according to research.

- The company that manufactures the greatest number of women's dresses each year is Mattel. Barbie's got to wear something.

- The Royal Mail once launched a search for the owner of a set of traffic lights sent in the post.

- A coffin-shaped smokers' booth has been placed outside an office in Manchester in a bid to discourage workers from lighting up.

- McDonald's is turning off its trademark golden arches in New Zealand, in response to a nationwide campaign to cut electricity use by 10%.

- Mailmen in Russia now carry revolvers after a recent decision by the government.

──────── **BUSINESS AND COMMERCE** ────────

- The first naked flight carried 87 passengers from Miami, Florida, to Cancun in Mexico.

- Fast-food provider Hardee's has recently introduced the Monster Thickburger. It has 1,420 calories and 107 grams of fat.

- Rizla has developed transparent tobacco rolling papers that are less than half as thin as a fine human hair.

- A Seattle taxi driver has vowed to continue wearing an Elvis-style cape for work despite being fined for breaking a dress code.

- A struggling teashop owner in China lured customers by placing lonely heart advertisements seeking a lover and then fixing the rendezvous in her cafe.

- A Georgia company will mix your loved one's ashes with cement and drop it into the ocean to form an artificial reef.

- Tartan kilts have become fashionable in Austria after archaeologists claimed the country invented them.

- A Norwegian witch has won a £5,000 business grant from her government to make and sell magic potions.

---------- **BUSINESS AND COMMERCE** ----------

- Ikea once apologised after accidentally naming a child's bunk bed after an obscene German expression. The wooden bed is called the 'Gutvik' which means 'Good f★★★' in German.

- One in three workers has come close to leaving their job because of the irritating habits of their colleagues, according to a survey.

- The busiest shopping hour of the Christmas season is between 3 p.m. and 4 p.m. on Christmas Eve.

- Sharwoods brought out a new range of curry sauces named Bundh and then realised the name translates as 'arse'.

- A Romanian taxi driver says his business has swelled since he started playing porn films in his cab for customers.

- China is the world's largest market for BMW's top-of-the-range 760Li. This car sells for £100,000 in China – more than almost all people in China make in a lifetime.

- Premiership footballers' favourite car has been revealed as the BMW X5, with 48 players owning the model.

BUSINESS AND COMMERCE

- The New York City subway system, in an effort to raise revenue, is considering selling sponsorships of individual stations to corporations. Riders could soon be getting off at Nike Grand Central Station or Sony Times Square.

- The average child recognises over 200 company logos by the time he enters primary school.

- The chip shop which came up with the deep-fried Mars Bar has launched another delicacy – fish in a Rice Krispie batter.

- The Nike swoosh was designed by a Portland State University student, and purchased by Nike for £18.

- Newscaster Sir Trevor MacDonald is exactly the kind of person drivers would trust to buy a new car from, according to a new survey.

- A US fizzy drinks manufacturer has issued an apology to its customers after failing to keep up with demand for its new product – Turkey and Gravy soda.

- One in four homeless people in South Korea has a credit card.

--------- **BUSINESS AND COMMERCE** ---------

- Monks in Wisconsin have set up their own online firm selling inkjet print cartridges.

- A 68-year-old US health-food executive served a 15-month sentence for labelling a 530-calorie doughnut as low-fat.

- A Russian telecoms company offers free phone calls to the White House for anyone who wants to rant at George Bush.

- Iceland consumes more Coca-Cola per capita than any other nation.

- A company in Warwickshire complained to trading standards after a 'slim, attractive' stripogram they booked turned out to be a 20-stone woman.

- They have square watermelons in Japan... they stack better.

- A mobile-telephone number in Bahrain is on sale for £10,000 – the number is 9111119.

INJURIES AND ILLNESSES

─────── **INJURIES AND ILLNESSES** ───────

- In 1992, 5,840 people checked into US emergency rooms with 'pillow-related injuries'.

- In 1994, there were over 420,000 accidents caused by kitchen knives, 122 thousand by drinking glasses, 29,000 by refrigerators, and 7,000 by dishwashers.

- A study published in a 1995 issue of the *Journal of Urology* estimated that 600,000 men in the United States are impotent from injuries to their crotches, about 40% of them from too-vigorous bicycling.

- Pain is measured in units of 'dols'. The instrument used to measure pain is a 'dolorimeter'.

- The number-one cause of blindness in the United States is diabetes.

- About 8,000 Americans are injured by musical instruments each year.

- The earliest form of electric shock treatment involved electric eels.

- Over 90% of diseases are caused or complicated by stress.

- If it is a drug, it has a side-effect.

INJURIES AND ILLNESSES

- In 1898, Bayer was advertising cough medicine containing heroin. Heroin used to be a cough medicine for children. A German company (Bayer) registered the word as a trademark.

- The oldest-known disease in the world is leprosy.

- Some arthritis medicine has gold salts which is used as an anti-inflammatory.

- In the 1800s, it was believed that gin could cure stomach problems.

- Sixty-five per cent of adolescents get acne.

- An 80-year-old London woman had a gall stone removed which weighed 13lb 14oz.

- Seventeenth-century hangover cures included flogging and bleeding by leeches.

- There is no leading cause of death for people who live past the age of 100.

- President Teddy Roosevelt died from an 'infected tooth'.

- The first open heart surgery was performed in 1893.

————INJURIES AND ILLNESSES————

- Breast reduction is the most common plastic surgery performed on American men.

- The flu pandemic of 1918 killed more than 20 million people.

- Cerumen is the medical term for earwax.

- During a kiss, as many as 278 bacteria colonies are exchanged.

- The average American kid catches six colds a year, the average kid in daycare catches ten.

- In 1992, 2,421 people checked into US emergency rooms with injuries involving houseplants.

- In 1990, in Hartsville, Tennessee, a 64-year old woman entered a hospital for surgery for what doctors diagnosed as a tumour on her buttocks. What surgeons found, however, was a four-inch pork chop bone, which they removed. They estimated that it had been in place for five to ten years.

- In the summer of 1998, 470 Chinese people were injured by spontaneously exploding beer bottles.

INJURIES AND ILLNESSES

- Travis Bogumill, a construction worker in Eau Claire, Wisconsin, was shot with a nail gun that drove a 3½-inch nail all the way into his skull. He was not killed, not even knocked unconscious. The only result from the incident was a decrease in his mathematics skills.

- Barbers at one time combined shaving and haircutting with bloodletting and pulling teeth. The white stripes on a field of red that spiral down a barber pole represent the bandages used in the bloodletting.

- [I]s already known that Viagra can cause a form of [tem]porary colour-blindness. But recent evidence [indi]cates that for some people it might also be the cause [th]at are essentially strokes in the eyes, causing [perma]nent damage to optic nerves, and thus permanent [loss of] vision.

- [Second]hand smoke from pipes and cigars is equally as [dangerou]s the smoke from cigarettes, if not more so.

- [In t]wo in 1,000 cases where a patient is [anaesthetise]d, the patient will awaken and be mentally [alert and fee]l all the pain of the surgery, but be paralysed [and unable to] signal or communicate with the doctors.

INJURIES AND ILLNESSES

- In a 1930 Quebec Junior Amateur Game, goalie Abie Goldberry was hit by a flying puck that ignited a pack of matches in his pocket, setting his uniform on fire. He was badly burned before his teammates could put the fire out.

- Despite the many rat-infested slums in New York City, rats bite only 311 people in an average year. But 1,519 residents are bitten annually by other New Yorkers.

- The two steps at the top and the two at the bottom are the four most dangerous steps in a staircase.

- An Austrian woman who hid behind her boyfriend's articulated lorry so she could jump out and surprise him was taken to hospital after he reversed over her.

- Over 11,000 people are injured every year trying out new sexual positions.

- A Cuban man was struck by lightning for the fifth time in 22 years.

- In the US, 55,700 people are injured by jewellery each year.

- A Thai man who held the record for spending time with snakes died after being bitten by a mamba.

──────INJURIES AND ILLNESSES──────

- Every year, 2,700 surgical patients go home from the hospital with metal tools, sponges and other objects left inside them. In 2000, 57 people died as a result of these mistakes.

- On an average day in the United States, about 40 people are hurt on trampolines.

- Second-hand smoke contains over 4,000 chemicals including more than 40 cancer-causing compounds.

- Once a person is totally buried by an avalanche, there is only a one in three chance of survival.

- Three hundred people report to emergency rooms across the country every day due to rollerblading accidents.

- A deliveryman from Ealing crashed his van two hours after his bosses gave him a safe driving award.

- Every year, over 8,800 people injure themselves with a toothpick.

- Student Robert Ricketts, 19, had his head bloodied when a train struck him. He told police he was trying to see how close to the moving train he could place his head without getting hit.

──────INJURIES AND ILLNESSES──────

- Several well-documented instances have been reported of extremely obese people flushing aircraft toilets while still sitting on them. The vacuum action of these toilets sucked the rectum inside out.

- An 83-year-old Canadian woman was rescued after spending two days wedged behind her toilet.

- Second-hand smoke contains twice as much ta? nicotine per unit volume as does smoke inha? cigarette. It contains 3 times as much cance? benzpyrene, 5 times as much carbon mon? times as much ammonia.

- A woman came home to find her hu? kitchen shaking frantically with wh? running from his waist towards th? Intending to jolt him away from? whacked him with a handy pl? door, breaking his arm in tw? he had been happily listenir?

- Two West German moto? in heavy fog near the ? was driving slowly n? moment of impact? windows. Both m? injuries. Their c?

INJURIES AND ILLNESSES

- After assassinating President Lincoln, John Wilkes Booth jumped to the stage. As he jumped, he tripped over an American flag and broke his leg.

- According to the US Department of Transportation, an average of 550 sleep-related highway accidents occur per day.

- Nearly 60% of accidents involving pedestrians aged under five happen in their own driveway when a vehicle backs over them.

- Of all the medicines available on the international market today, 7% are fake. In some countries, the figure for counterfeit medicines can be as high as 50%.

- Lead paint – linked to serious kidney problems, brain damage and learning disabilities – is found in 75% of all homes, not just old, rundown houses.

- The US tops the world in plastic-surgery procedures. Next is Mexico.

- According to a Boston study of 87,000 female nurses, those who ate five or more servings of carrots a week were 68% less likely to suffer a stroke than those who seldom ate carrots.

INJURIES AND ILLNESSES

- 1 in every 200 people is a psychopath and they look just like everyone else.

- In medieval Japan, dentists extracted teeth with their hands.

- Mark Twain (Samuel Clemens) thought fasting was a cure for illness. He would cure his colds and fevers by not eating for one or two days.

- Ancient Egyptians believed eating fried mice would cure a toothache.

- Austrian physician Alfred Adler theorised that people are primarily motivated to overcome inherent feelings of inferiority. He coined the term 'sibling rivalry'.

- One of the first anaesthetics was used to help surgeons, not patients. It was developed by the Ancient Incas of Peru over 1,000 years ago. While they worked, Inca surgeons chewed leaves of the coca plant to calm their nerves. We now know these leaves contain a powerful painkilling drug.

- A Massachusetts surgeon left a patient with an open incision for 35 minutes while he went to deposit a cheque.

INJURIES AND ILLNESSES

- Lead poisoning was common among upper-class Romans who used lead-sweetened wine and leaded grape pulp as a condiment.

- Over 2,500 left-handed people are killed each year, because they used products made for right-handed people.

HUMAN BODY

——————— **HUMAN BODY** ———————

- There are nine muscles in your ear.

- The navel divides the body of a newborn baby into two equal parts.

- If the average male never shaved, his beard would be 13ft long when he died.

- Experts say the human body has 60,000 miles of blood vessels.

- The human eye blinks an average of 4,200,000 times a year.

- Foetuses can hiccup.

- Your brain uses 40% of the oxygen that enters your bloodstream.

- Your left hand does an average of 56% of your typing.

- Men without hair on their chests are more likely to get cirrhosis of the liver than men with hair.

- Blood is about 78% water.

- The longest recorded sneezing fit lasted 978 days.

──────── HUMAN BODY ────────

- Sunburn seems to heal in just a few days, but the blood vessels under the skin do not return to their normal condition for up to 15 months.

- We lose half a litre of water a day through breathing.

- The screaming of an upset baby can damage your hearing. Kids can scream at levels up to 90 dB, and permanent damage can be caused at 85 dB.

- Your stomach has 35 million digestive glands.

- At the moment of conception, you spent about half an hour as a single cell.

- There are about one trillion bacteria on each of your feet.

- Side by side, 2,000 cells from the human body could cover about one square inch.

- Your body contains about 4oz of salt.

- Injured fingernails grow faster than uninjured ones.

HUMAN BODY

- Jeffrey and Sheryl McGowen in Houston turned to vitro fertilisation. Two eggs were implanted in Sheryl's womb, and both of them split. Sheryl gave birth to two sets of identical twins at once.

- If you calculated the DNA length for each person, it would stretch across the diameter of the solar system.

- Twelve per cent of the British population are left handed.

- The average heart beats 2.5 billion times in a lifetime.

- It is a medical fact that, after drinking, the last place in the body to be cleared of alcohol is the brain. We often stumble and drop things because our bodies and brains are out of synch.

- Even mild dehydration will slow down one's metabolism as much as 3%.

- When you are looking at someone you love, your pupils dilate; they do the same when you are looking at someone you hate.

- It takes twice as long to lose new muscle if you stop working out as it did to gain it.

HUMAN BODY

- The three things pregnant women dream most of during their first trimester are frogs, worms and potted plants.

- 55% of people yawn within five minutes of seeing someone else yawn. Reading about yawning makes most people yawn.

- Your skin weighs about 3.2kg.

- A blink lasts approximately 0.3 seconds.

- Seventy-five per cent of Americans are chronically dehydrated.

- In 37% of Americans, the thirst mechanism is so weak that it is often mistaken for hunger.

- A mere 2% drop in body water can trigger fuzzy short-term memory, trouble with basic math, and difficulty focusing on the computer screen or on a printed page.

- The lifespan of a taste bud is ten days.

- We forget 80% of what we learn every day.

- Men get hiccups more often than women do.

——————— HUMAN BODY ———————

- In 1991, the average bra size in the United States was 34B. Today it's 36C.

- The average North Korean seven-year-old is almost three inches shorter than the average South Korean seven-year-old.

- The Amish diet is high in meat, dairy, refined sugars and calories. Yet obesity is virtually unknown among them. The difference is, since they have no TVs, cars or powered machines, they spend their time in manual labour.

- The most common phobia in the world is odynophobia which is the fear of pain.

- In a University of Arizona study, rails and armrests in public buses were found to be contaminated by the highest concentration of bodily fluids.

- A man named Charles Osborne had the hiccups for 69 years.

- An average human loses about 200 head hairs per day.

- Mexican women spend 15.3% of their life in ill health.

HUMAN BODY

- In 2004, one in six girls in the United States entered puberty at age eight. A hundred years ago, only one in a hundred entered puberty that early.

- Your body gives off enough heat in 30 minutes to bring half a gallon of water to a boil.

- You use over 70 muscles to say one word.

- Bone is stronger, inch for inch, than the steel in skyscrapers.

- About one-third of the human race has 20-20 vision.

- In a hot climate, you can sweat as much as three gallons of water a day.

- Everyone is colour-blind at birth.

- Fingernails are made from the same substance as a bird's beak.

- A runner consumes about seven quarts of oxygen while running a 100-yard dash.

- Your teeth start growing six months before you are born.

HUMAN BODY

- Your big toes have two bones each while the rest have three.

- A pair of human feet contains 250,000 sweat glands.

- Living brain cells are bright pink.

- Your ears secrete more earwax when you are afraid than when you aren't.

- Your body uses 300 muscles to balance itself when you are standing still.

- If saliva cannot dissolve something, you cannot taste it.

- Your body contains the same amount of iron as an iron nail.

- You will have to walk 80km for your legs to equal the amount of exercise your eyes get daily.

- It takes about 20 seconds for a red blood cell to circle the whole body.

- Humans are born with 300 bones but, by the time they reach adulthood, they only have 206.

—— HUMAN BODY ——

- The right lung in humans is slightly larger than the left.

- The average woman is 5in shorter than the average man is.

- The heart beats about 100,000 times each day.

- Fidgeting can burn about 350 calories a day.

- A shank is the part of the sole between the heel and the ball of the foot.

- The talus is the second largest bone in the foot.

- The attachment of human muscles to skin is what causes dimples.

- A 13-year-old child found a tooth growing out of his foot in 1977.

- A woman's heart beats faster than a man's does.

- Another name for your little or pinky finger is Wanus.

- Dogs and humans are the only animals with prostates.

- It only takes 7lb of pressure to rip off your ears.

HUMAN BODY

- Wearing headphones for just one hour will multiply the number of bacteria in your ear 700 times.

- If you sneeze too hard, you can fracture a rib. If you try to suppress a sneeze, you can rupture a blood vessel in your head or neck and die.

- The total surface area of a pair of human lungs is equal to that of a tennis court.

- It takes the food seven seconds to get from your mouth to your stomach.

- You can only smell 1/20th as well as a dog.

- The average human dream lasts two to three seconds.

- Human thighbones are stronger than concrete.

- The tooth is the only part of the human body that can't repair itself.

THE ANIMAL
KINGDOM

THE ANIMAL KINGDOM

- Monkeys fling faeces at each other when agitated.

- Ravens can learn to open a box to get a treat, and then teach others to do the same.

- Cockroaches can find their way in a dark room by dragging one antenna against the wall.

- A Brazilian MP has drawn up a new law to ban people from giving their pets 'human' names.

- Finches practise songs in their sleep.

- Crickets hear through their knees.

- A Chinese man has trained his pet dog to walk on its hind legs for up to five miles.

- The heart of a blue whale only beats nine times a minute.

- Baboons and chimps dig for clean water when the surface water is polluted. Chimps even use sticks as digging tools.

- A weddell seal can hold its breath for seven hours.

THE ANIMAL KINGDOM

- Conservation workers have introduced an exercise regime for giant pandas in Chinese zoos because they're too fat to mate.

- Turkeys were first brought to Britain in 1526 by Yorkshireman William Strickland, who sold six, acquired from American Indians, for sixpence each in Bristol.

- The Basenji, an African dog, is the only dog that does not bark.

- One in three dog owners say they have talked to their pets on the phone.

- A Belgian company is producing ice cream specifically for dogs.

- A course that teaches people how to perform the kiss of life on dogs has been launched in Chile.

- A church in Connecticut is giving Holy Communion to pets and offering them special worship services.

- Chimps live in groups that each has its own culture.

- The average American dog will cost its owner £9,000 in its lifetime.

---------- **THE ANIMAL KINGDOM**----------

- Only male turkeys gobble. Females make a clicking sound.

- The average pregnancy of an Indian elephant lasts 650 days.

- A geriatric dwarf mouse that lives at a university in Michigan has become the world's oldest after celebrating his fourth birthday.

- A Swiss woman is offering lessons on how to talk with animals for £360 a time.

- The red kangaroo can produce two different types of milk at the same time from adjacent teats to feed both younger and older offspring.

- Firefighters in Florida are carrying oxygen masks for cats, dogs and even hamsters to help save pets suffering from smoke inhalation.

- Cows drink anywhere from 25 to 50 gallons of water each day.

- A German basset hound with the longest dog ears in the world has had them insured for £30,000.

—————— THE ANIMAL KINGDOM——————

- Hard rock music makes termites chew through wood at twice their usual speed. ✓

- Red squirrels are being given rope bridges to help them cross busy roads in Formby, Merseyside.

- A Michigan woman who runs a boutique for pets is stocking a special range of Halloween costumes for dogs. ✓

- Domestic turkeys cannot fly because of their size and breeding but, in the wild, they can fly at up to 50mph over short distances and run at 20mph.

- The Giant African cricket enjoys eating human hair.

- The first known 'zeedonks' were the result of an accidental mating between a male Chapman's zebra and a female black ass (donkey) at Colchester Zoo in 1983.

- Ziggy, the largest and oldest elephant ever in captivity, was taught to play 'Yes, Sir, that's my baby' on the harmonica.

- Ninety-five per cent of the creatures on earth are smaller than a chicken egg. ✓

THE ANIMAL KINGDOM

- The Antarctic notothenia fish has a protein in its blood that acts like antifreeze and stops the fish freezing in icy sea.

- Goat's eyes have rectangular pupils.

- The megalodon shark became extinct about 1.6 million years ago. Marine biologists have estimated the megalodon shark was double the size and weight of today's great white shark.

- Catfish are the only animals that naturally have an odd number of whiskers.

- Sheep can detect other sheep faces in the way that humans do. Researchers claim they can remember up to 50 sheep faces.

- Male bats have the highest rate of homosexuality of any mammal.

- When mating, a hummingbird's wings beat 200 times a second.

- A cow gives nearly 200,000 glasses of milk in her lifetime

- The average American bald eagle weighs about 9lb.

THE ANIMAL KINGDOM

- Robins eat three miles of earthworms in a year.

- The beautiful Cone Shell Molluscs are just 2in long but have a deadly poison-filled harpoon-like tooth that spears their prey, injecting it with lethal toxins.

- A study has concluded that if a woodchuck could chuck wood it could chuck about 700lb.

- Baby elephants can drink over 80 litres of milk a day.

- An experiment in Canada determined that chickens lay most eggs when pop music is played.

- A cow has four stomachs.

- Two dogs were hanged for witchcraft during the Salem witch trials.

- All polar bears are left-handed.

- A mother shark can give birth to as many as 70 baby sharks per litter.

- The top speed of a pigeon in flight is 90mph.

- An adult crocodile can go two years without eating.

THE ANIMAL KINGDOM

- Emus cannot walk backwards.

- The oldest bird on record was Cocky, a cockatoo, who died in London Zoo at the age of 82.

- A chicken's top speed is 9mph.

- Both gorillas and housecats purr.

- Ostriches can run faster than horses and the males can roar like lions.

- Squirrels cannot see the colour red.

- If birds could sweat, they wouldn't be able to fly.

- The decapitated jaws of a snapping turtle can keep snapping for about a day.

- Jackrabbits got their name because their ears look like a donkey's (Jackass).

- Sheep can survive up to two weeks buried in snowdrifts.

- The last animal in the dictionary is the zyzzyva, a tropical American weevil.

THE ANIMAL KINGDOM

- The giraffe has the highest blood pressure of any animal.

- Armadillos can catch malaria.

- Baboons cannot throw overhand.

- Lions are the only cats that live in packs.

- To get a gallon of milk, it takes about 345 squirts from a cow's udder.

- A warthog has only four warts, all of which are on its head.

- The penalty for stealing a rabbit in 19th-century England was seven years in prison.

- Even bloodhounds cannot smell the difference between identical twins.

- Cows and cats both get hairballs.

- Camels are born without humps.

- Anteaters can flick their tongues 160 times a minute.

- Chimpanzees will hunt ducks if given the opportunity.

THE ANIMAL KINGDOM

- Black sheep have a better sense of smell than white sheep.

- Whales and buffalos both stampede.

- A hibernating bear can go as long as six months without a toilet break.

- A bat can eat up to 1,000 insects per hour.

- Turkeys can reproduce without having sex. It's called parthenogenesis.

- Snakes have two sex organs.

- Male rhesus monkeys often hang from tree branches by their amazing prehensile penises.

- The English sparrow is not a sparrow and it comes from Africa, not England.

- One humped camels run faster than two humped camels.

- A blue whale's testicles are the size of a family car.

- Skunks can accurately spray their fluid up to 10ft.

THE ANIMAL KINGDOM

- Sheep snore.

- To maintain a chimpanzee in captivity for 60 years it would cost an estimated £200,000.

- An ant can detect movement through 5cm of earth.

- Lobsters like to eat lobster.

- The only time a turkey whistles is when it is panicking.

- A group of jellyfish is called a 'smack'.

- Camel hairbrushes are made from squirrel hair.

- Sloths sneeze slowly. They also give birth upside down slowly.

- A hippo can open its mouth wide enough to fit a 4ft child inside.

- A parrot that shouts 'Show us your t*ts' at women on board a Royal Navy ship is always taken ashore during royal visits.

- The Andrex puppy has met a waxwork copy of itself at Madame Tussauds in London.

THE ANIMAL KINGDOM

- A dog just over 7in long and weighing 27oz has been officially confirmed as the world's smallest living dog.

- Deer urine can turn blue when they become dehydrated in the winter.

- Cash-strapped bosses at Moscow Zoo are renting out animals for the day in a bid to boost funds.

- The London Zoo employs an 'entertainment director' for the animals.

- A German pot-bellied pig called Berta has passed an audition to star in an opera.

- A lonely and confused male flamingo has caused a stir at a Gloucestershire nature reserve by trying to incubate a pebble.

- Hook-tip moth caterpillars defend their territories by drumming out warnings.

- Chinese scientists are appealing to the Guinness Book of Records to recognise a 900kg pig which died earlier this month as the biggest ever porker.

———————— **THE ANIMAL KINGDOM** ————————

- Fish are much brainier than previously thought – and can learn quicker than dogs.

- A Chilean doctor is using alternative medicines to treat pets and their owners for mental conditions including depression.

- A Brazilian vet is offering plastic surgery and botox injections for pampered pets.

- Two polar bears have turned green at Singapore Zoo as a result of algae growing in their hair.

- The world's first restaurant for cats is about to open in New York.

- Moscow Zoo keepers are to fit televisions in the cages of their gorillas in a bid to make them 'think more'.

- Rescuers did a microchip scan on a stray cat that was wandering the streets of Oxford and found it had been registered in the USA.

- Scientists say they want to send 15 mice into space to help prepare for possible human missions to Mars.

THE ANIMAL KINGDOM

- Conveners of an Australian agricultural show are so concerned at the rise of cosmetic surgery among cattle breeders that they have issued new rules forbidding it.

- A chicken farm in Germany is claiming a new world record after a hen laid a giant egg weighing 6oz.

- A German businessman who trained his dog to do the Hitler salute was given 13 months' probation.

- Croat farmers staged a beauty contest for goats in a bid to publicise the fact that traditional goat farming is dying out.

- A Catholic priest has started holding masses for pets in the German city of Cologne.

- A German zoo has scrapped plans to break up homosexual penguin couples following protests from gay-rights groups.

- A Brazilian seaside town has built two toilets for dogs to try to stop pets fouling the beach.

- If an entire family is overweight, it is likely that the dog will be too.

———— **THE ANIMAL KINGDOM** ————

- Homing pigeons are becoming increasingly lost because of mobile-phone masts, say racing enthusiasts.

- A Japanese researcher claims dogs can sense earthquakes before they happen.

- A Brazilian man who bought a 6ft boa constrictor online faces charges after it was posted to him in a paper box.

- Ptarmigans help their chicks go out into the world by teaching them which plants are more nutritious.

- A goldfish believed to be the world's oldest in captivity is still swimming strongly – 44 years after it was won at a fairground.

- A marathon runner became the first human to win a horse-against-man race in the event's 25-year history.

- A Brazilian company is launching a chewing gum for dogs.

- The Amazon River is home to the world's only nut- and seed-eating fish.

- An elderly elephant in Thailand has been given a new lease of life after being fitted with custom-made dentures.

THE ANIMAL KINGDOM

- New Zealand has abandoned plans for a flatulence tax on animals in the face of fierce opposition from farmers.

- A sea-hare can lay 40,000 eggs in one minute.

- A three-year-old boxer is being dubbed the most allergic dog in the UK after being found to suffer severe allergies to grass, flowers, cotton, lamb, soya, white fish and most materials used in bedding.

- China has built a biscuit factory to cater exclusively for the nutritional needs of its captive giant pandas.

- British dog owners spend an average of £981 a year on their animals while cat owners shell out £476, researchers have concluded.

- A gozzard is a person who owns geese.

- A zoo in Russia is claiming a world record after a hippopotamus named Mary gave birth for the 24th time at the age of 47.

- The UK's first canine classroom assistant has been appointed to a school in Derbyshire.

- Armadillos get an average of 18.5 hours of sleep per day.

──────── **THE ANIMAL KINGDOM**────────

● Giving postmen training in dog psychology has reduced attacks on them by 80%, the German post office is claiming.

● A gym exclusively for dogs has opened in Santiago, Chile.

● When snakes are born with two heads, they fight each other for food.

● A zoo in India is serving brandy to bears to keep them warm in winter.

● Chocolate affects a dog's heart and nervous system; a few ounces are enough to kill a small dog.

● A flock of swallows have delayed more than 100 flights after taking over a runway at Beijing International Airport.

● A Canadian scientist claims to have proven that the world's most expensive coffee really does taste better because the beans it is produced from have been eaten and defecated by a wild cat.

THE ANIMAL KINGDOM

- Former First Division footballer, ex-Crystal Palace and Middlesbrough defender Craig Harrison says he has dozens of dogs on a waiting list after opening a hydrotherapy pool for overweight hounds.

- The UK faces an invasion of parakeets, with the wild population likely to exceed 100,000 in a decade, experts are warning.

- Male and female rats may have sex twenty times a day.

- Rabbits love liquorice.

- An Essex man believes he has the biggest cockerel in Britain – a 2ft monster which he calls Melvin.

- Farm animals have been banned from council flats in Kiev after a survey found residents were keeping more than 3,000 pigs, 500 cows and 1,000 goats.

- Mosquitoes have teeth.

- Penguins can jump as high as 6 feet in the air.

- Scottish scientists have become the first in the world to breed a golden eagle chick from frozen sperm.

THE ANIMAL KINGDOM

- A snake measuring more than 19ft long and weighing almost 16 stone was found inside a factory in Brazil.

- Polar bears' fur is not white, it's clear. Polar bear skin is actually black. Their hair is hollow and acts like fibre optics, directing sunlight to warm their skin.

- Italy has put border collies, corgis and St Bernards on a dangerous-dogs list that bans children and criminals from owning them.

- Princess Tamara Borbon and her five-year-old Yorkshire terrier Bugsy were top of the bill at a canine fashion show at Harrods.

- Thailand's prime minister has banned vagrant elephants from the streets of Bangkok in an effort to ease traffic chaos.

- A Japanese department store is cashing in on a pet boom by offering a special £145 New Year meal for dogs.

- Canada's entry in the world's most prestigious international art exhibition features a video filmed by a Jack Russell puppy called Stanley.

———————— **THE ANIMAL KINGDOM** ————————

- Trained hawks employed to keep pigeons from making a mess on visitors in a Manhattan park were grounded in August 2003 because one of the birds mistook a Chihuahua for its lunch.

- A British homing pigeon has become a star in the US after completing a 3,321-mile journey across the Atlantic.

- Giant rats have been trained to sniff out landmines in Tanzania.

- Most marine fish can survive in a tank filled with human blood.

- Most cows give more milk when they listen to music.

- Poodles, dachshunds and Chihuahuas have strutted down the catwalk at a fashion show organised by a Tokyo department store.

- Some dogs can predict when a child will have an epileptic seizure, and even protect the child from injury. They're not trained to do this, but simply learn to respond after observing at least one attack.

THE ANIMAL KINGDOM

- Rats destroy an estimated third of the world's food supply each year.

- The United States has never lost a war in which mules were used.

- International animal-rights groups are urging Thailand to ban orang-utan kickboxing fights that are being staged at a Bangkok safari park.

- A chain of gyms in the US has started offering yoga classes for dogs.

- The world's only robotic swimming shark is moving into an aquarium with four live sharks. The 2m-long creature called Roboshark2 will spend up to three years alongside sand tiger sharks at the National Marine Aquarium in Plymouth.

- Armadillos breed in July, but get pregnant in November after delaying implantation. This allows the young to be born during the spring when there is an abundance of food.

- The world's smallest winged insect is the Tanzanian parasitic wasp. It's smaller than the eye of a housefly.

THE ANIMAL KINGDOM

- In Tokyo, they sell wigs for dogs.

- Tarantulas can go up to two years without eating or drinking. Sea turtles can go up to 35 years without eating or drinking.

- Manatees possess vocal chords that give them the ability to speak like humans, but they don't do so because they have no ears with which to hear the sound.

- Homing pigeons use roads where possible to help find their way home.

- Authorities in New Delhi are planning to export cow dung and urine to the United States. The dung will be processed into compost while the urine will be converted into a biopesticide.

- Engineers in the East Midlands are fitting rubber boots to the top of pylons to save squirrels from electrocution and keep the power flowing.

NEWS HEADLINES

—————— NEWS HEADLINES ——————

- Blondes perform intelligence tests more slowly after reading jokes playing on their supposed stupidity

- A German-based doctor has invented breast implants made from titanium.

- A Warwickshire woman married a man just a month after he stabbed her for having pre-wedding jitters. ✓

- A pillow designed in the shape of a woman's lap has become one of the best-selling Christmas gifts in Japan.

- An Englishman who shot himself in the groin was jailed for five years for illegal possession of a firearm. ✓

- A New York woman reportedly fended off her husband's violent sexual advances by setting him on fire.

- Landlords have found the best way to get rid of drinkers at closing time at Christmas is to play a Cliff Richard ✓ song.

- A Chilean woman was horrified when she received a box through the post with a human brain inside it.

- A judge in America is reportedly facing the sack after using a penis pump while trying cases in court.

———————— **NEWS HEADLINES** ————————

- Archaeologists have dug up a 1,000-year-old padded bra in China.

- An Iranian man who struck a suicide pact with his new bride over their guilt for having pre-marital sex is being held by police after he backed out of his side of the bargain.

- Investors in Berlin are building Germany's first gay and lesbian old people's home.

- Thieves who stole a public toilet in the Belarus city of Gomel accidentally kidnapped a man still locked inside.

- A university student is auctioning his virginity on his personal website and has put a reserve of £6,000 on it.

- A female student came home to find a drunken burglar in her apartment, wearing her clothes.

- A clinic at Albury in southern New South Wales has been given permission to advertise overseas for fully paid holidays to Australia for sperm donors.

- A Russian oil company has won a rare legal victory when a court ruled it could sell cannabis vodka.

——————————— **NEWS HEADLINES** ———————————

- A Romanian man faces charges that he tried to blow up his kitchen because his wife was a lousy cook. ✓

- Residents of an Austrian village called F*cking have voted against changing the name.

- A German man who faked his death so he could leave his family for a younger woman has been fined £9,000.

- Police believe a US teenager who crashed a car into a telegraph pole was having sex with his girlfriend at the time.

- Shepherds in the Scottish highlands could be given free Viagra to halt a drastic drop in their numbers.

- Croatian monks have been ordered to sell off their BMWs and Mercedes

- Romanian doctors have removed a man's wedding ring from his penis.

- A female panda named Hua Mei is pregnant after watching hours of videos showing other pandas mating.

- Subbuteo fans can now buy male and female streakers for their game.

─── NEWS HEADLINES ───

- Two San Francisco police officers have been caught moonlighting in a hardcore-porn movie.

- Prostitutes in a Dutch city say their business is being ruined by policemen turning up to watch them have sex with clients.

- A Buddhist monk decided to break his lifelong vow of celibacy with a prostitute, but picked up an undercover police officer instead.

- A company manufacturing skin cream from snail extract is exporting 20,000 bottles to the US every month.

- A mayor who set up a direct hotline for people to call with civic problems is asking bored housewives to stop inviting him round for sex.

- Scientists in Australia have found that rotten bananas could provide enough energy for 500 homes.

- A Serbian tie maker is planning to launch a new range of penis cravats for the man who has everything.

- A Danish company has given its employees free subscriptions to internet pornography sites.

——————— NEWS HEADLINES ———————

- Police in Germany had to rescue a swimming-pool attendant at a hen party after the bride-to-be tried to bully him into having sex.

- A groom has been given away at his wedding by his ex-wife – and his best man was his ex's new boyfriend.

- A Romanian father-of-five needed medical help after he superglued a condom to his penis.

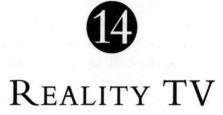

14

REALITY TV

──────── REALITY TV ────────

- Simon Cowell reportedly made $2 million hosting 2002's *American Idol*.

- Ex-Take That singer Mark Owen won *Celebrity Big Brother* and relaunched his music career – but after one top-ten single his comeback stalled and he was dumped by his record label.

- There are 36 cameras in the *Big Brother* house following the housemates' every move. ✓

- *Survivor* first aired as *Expedition Robinson* in Sweden in 1997.

- A German TV station wants men for a reality show in which they'd learn how to win estranged partners back.

- Items banned from the *Big Brother* house include writing materials, mobile phones, radios, walkmans, CDs or CD players, computers, PDAs (Psion, Palm Pilot, etc), calendars, clocks and watches, drugs and narcotics, personal medication (except in consultation with *Big Brother*), weapons, any electronic equipment or items requiring batteries and clothes with prominent logos.

- Simon Cowell dropped out of school at the age of 16.

——————————— REALITY TV ———————————

• A Brazilian woman is suing a TV station for the trauma she suffered after being caught up in a reconstruction of a kidnapping. The lady, from Sao Paulo, thought it was a real incident and crashed her car into a truck as she tried to escape.

• A Slovenian TV programme that tried to prove top models were brainless bimbos was scrapped after a beauty queen turned out to have a higher IQ than a nuclear physicist.

• Over the course of a *Big Brother* series, around 2,000 radio mic batteries will be used in the house.

• Creator Charlie Parsons originally pitched *Survivor* to ABC in the early 1990s but, without a pilot, they passed on the idea. Today, there are approximately 20 countries producing their own homegrown versions of *Survivor*.

• A reality show has been launched in Brazil to try to find the new Pele.

• The US version of *Big Brother* may have been a flop, but the show was so popular in Spain the winner had to be airlifted from the house as frenzied fans invaded the set.

————————— **REALITY TV** —————————

- An ambitious $40 million series called *Destination Mir* was to include launching contestants into outer space. But, after the Russian space station was ditched recently, NBC said the show – now called *Destination Space* – was put on the back burner.

- Afraid he'd be portrayed as a fool, Sinisa Savija committed suicide after being the first contestant voted off *Expedition Robinson*, the Swedish version of *Survivor*, which aired on public television there in 1997.

- *The Real World* was originally conceived as St Mark's Place, a soap opera about young people in New York. But MTV balked at the cost, so creators Mary-Ellis Bunim and Jonathan Murray did some quick thinking and pitched the cheaper real-people angle. MTV thought the price was right and bought the idea on the spot.

- The UK *Big Brother* house is based in Elstree, Herts.

- Guests on *The Jerry Springer Show* have to sign contracts before they appear. One states that, if a guest isn't telling the truth, they could be liable for the cost of the show. If a guest is going on to find out a surprise they have to read and sign a list of 20 possible surprises ranging from a reunion to finding out that their partner is a man.

REALITY TV

- 50 kilometres of cable have been used in the technical construction of the *Big Brother* house.

- A Greek policeman was sacked after appearing on his country's version of *Pop Idol*.

- Each *Jerry Springer* talk show costs around $80,000 to make.

- Over the course of a series, around 10,000 hours of tape will be recorded from the *Big Brother* house.

- David Letterman is part owner of Team Rahal auto racing team.

- A US woman whose rescue from her car during floods was shown on national television was arrested by a policeman who remembered she was banned from driving.

- David Letterman funds a scholarship at Ball State University (his alma mater).

- Simon Cowell once worked as a mail boy at RCA.

- *The Jerry Springer Show* airs in over 150 markets.

——————————— **REALITY TV** ———————————

- Applicants for *Big Brother 3* went to incredible lengths to get noticed in their application videos. One man even pierced an intimate body part on screen while a bikini-clad woman stood on a central reservation with a sign saying: 'Beep if you want to see me on *Big Brother*'.

- *Candid Camera* began its life on radio as *Candid Microphone*.

- A Japanese man featured in a documentary about his religious pilgrimage was arrested after police recognised him as a suspect in a decade-old stabbing.

- As well as five manned cameras, producers in the *Big Brother* control room operate an additional 15 cameras fitted to remote-controlled pan and tilt head cameras located in the house. A further 13 fixed cameras ensure that every area of the house and garden is under surveillance.

- A Court TV poll showed 87.3% of respondents think the outcome of the original *Survivor* was manipulated.

- One couple on *Temptation Island* was recently removed from the land of debauchery when it was revealed that they have a one-and-a-half-year-old son. Fox TV did not want to be held responsible for the break-up of a family.

REALITY TV

- Online bookies Paddy Power gave initial odds for a transsexual winning *Big Brother* of 33/1.

- In *Big Brother 3*, there were seven chickens in total, comprising three different breeds: two Boveneras, two Exchequer Leghorns and three Little Red Hens.

- *America's Most Wanted* has helped apprehend 618 criminals.

FOOD AND DRINK

FOOD AND DRINK

- Americans buy 2.7 billion packages of breakfast cereal each year. If laid end to end, the empty cereal boxes from one year's consumption would stretch to the moon and back.

- The largest pumpkin pie ever made was over 5ft in diameter and weighed over 350lb.

- Smarties were launched as Chocolate Beans in 1937 by Rowntree of York. They were originally priced at 2d. (less than 1p). They were renamed Smarties and packed in the familiar tube one year later. A tube now sells for about 35p.

- More than ten million turkeys are eaten in Britain every Christmas – with nine out of ten people having it for dinner.

- The ONLY cure for a hangover is to drink alcohol. The most effective is champagne because it gets into the blood stream fastest. Warning: only one drink is needed to do the trick.

- In the 13th century, Europeans baptised children with beer.

————————FOOD AND DRINK————————

- The cereal industry uses 816 million pounds of sugar per year, enough to coat each and every American with more than three pounds of sugar. The cereal with the highest amount of sugar per serving is Smacks, which is 53% sugar.

- Weekend beer drinkers in Dublin consume 9,800 pints an hour between 5.30 p.m. Friday and 3 a.m. on Monday.

- The largest egg ever had five yolks and was 31cm around the long axis.

- In the 1820s, a temperance movement tried to ban coffee and nearly succeeded.

- Charles Lindbergh took only four sandwiches with him on his famous transatlantic flight.

- At one time, pumpkins were recommended for the removal of freckles and curing snakebites.

- When production of Smarties resumed after World War II, they were made with plain chocolate because of the shortage of milk.

————————— **FOOD AND DRINK** —————————

- Henry VIII was the first British king to eat turkey at Christmas but Edward VII made it fashionable.

- Acorns were used as a coffee substitute during the American Civil War.

- Boiled eggs are the most popular way to eat eggs in Britain, followed by scrambled and fried.

- Chocolate was used as medicine during the 18th century. It was believed that chocolate could cure a stomachache.

- Twenty-five per cent of the fish you eat are raised on fish farms.

- Each year, Americans use enough foam peanuts to fill ten 85-storey buildings.

- Americans consume about 10lb, or 160 bowls, of cereal per person each year. But America ranks only fourth in per capita cereal consumption. Ireland ranks first, England is second and Australia third.

- The biggest pumpkin in the world weighed 1,337.6lb.

- Bubble gum and candy floss were invented by dentists.

————————FOOD AND DRINK————————

- The longest sausage made in Australia was 6.9 miles long.

- Before Prohibition, the most common form of drinking beer at home was drinking it out of a bucket filled at a local pub or brewery.

- In the 1800s, people believed that gin could cure stomach problems.

- Fifty-eight per cent of American school kids say pizza is their favourite cafeteria food.

- McDonald's calls frequent buyers of their food heavy users.

- All fruits have three layers: exocarp (skin), mesocarp (pulp) and endocarp (pit).

- The chicken is one of the few things that can be eaten before it's born and after it's dead.

- Thirty-two out of 33 samples of well-known brands of milk purchased in Los Angeles and Orange counties in California had trace amounts of perchlorate, which is the explosive component in rocket fuel.

————————— FOOD AND DRINK —————————

● As a nation, Britain eats nearly 10 billion eggs a year; that's 26 million every day, which placed end to end would reach from the earth to the moon.

● Hershey's Kisses are called that because the machine that makes them looks like it's kissing the conveyor belt.

● Chocolate contains phenyl ethylamine, the same chemical that your brain produces when you fall in love.

● If you place a T-bone steak in a bowl of coke, it will be gone in two days.

● The heaviest egg weighed 454g – that's six times heavier than an average large egg from the shops.

● Pour a can of Coca-Cola into the toilet bowl and let the 'real thing' sit for one hour, then flush clean. The citric acid in Coke removes stains from vitreous china.

● There is a bar in London that sells vaporised vodka, which is inhaled instead of sipped.

● Before 1989, the dark-brown Smartie had a plain-chocolate centre and the light-brown one tasted of coffee.

FOOD AND DRINK

- To cure hangovers, boozers in the Middle Ages would down a plate of bitter almonds and dried eel after drinking.

- The world's oldest piece of chewing gum is 9,000 years old.

- The world's largest omelette was made in Madrid from 5,000 eggs by chef Carlos Fernandez. It weighed 1,320lb.

- The average American drinks 3.4 cups of coffee a day.

- The peach was the first fruit eaten on the moon.

- In the US, 49% of Americans start each morning with a bowl of cereal, 30% eat toast, 28% eat eggs, 28% have coffee, 17% have hot cereal and fewer than 10% have pancakes, sausage, bagels or french toast.

- In Outer Mongolia, drunks slurp down a pickled sheep's eye in tomato juice to stave off hangovers.

- The ancient Greeks slaughtered a sheep and ate its entrails while they were still warm.

─────────── **FOOD AND DRINK** ───────────

● The eight original colours of Smarties – red, orange, yellow, green, mauve, pink, light-brown and dark-brown – remained the same until the replacement of the light-brown one with a blue Smartie following a successful promotion in 1989. There have since been complaints that the colouring made children hyperactive.

● The Romans ate fried canaries – the ancient equivalent of our all-day-breakfast fry-up.

ROYALS

——————————— ROYALS ———————————

● 'I want to make certain that I have some plants left to
✗ talk to.'
   PRINCE CHARLES, OPENING THE MILLENNIUM SEED BANK

● 'You were playing your instruments, weren't you? Or do
   you have tape recorders under your seats?'
   PRINCE PHILIP, 'CONGRATULATING' A SCHOOL BAND ON
   THEIR PERFORMANCE IN AUSTRALIA, IN 2002

● 'Most people call their dogs Fergie. I'm kind of proud.
   You hear it in the park, "Fergie, come here."'
   SARAH FERGUSON, ON DOGS

● 'I talk too much about things of which I have never
   claimed any special knowledge; just contemplate the
   horrifying prospect if I were to get my teeth into
   something even remotely familiar.'
   PRINCE PHILIP

● 'A leper colony.'
   PRINCESS DIANA, ON THE ROYAL FAMILY

● 'Just as we can't blame people for their parents, we can't
   blame South America for not having been members of
   the British Empire.'
   PRINCE PHILIP, AT THE BRITISH AND
   LATIN CHAMBERS OF COMMERCE

ROYALS

● 'I expect a 30-year apprenticeship before I am king.'

PRINCE CHARLES

● 'I declare this thing open – whatever it is.'

PRINCE PHILIP, AT THE OPENING OF VANCOUVER CITY HALL'S NEW ANNEXE

● 'Sometimes as a bit of twit.'

PRINCE CHARLES, RESPONDING TO DAVID FROST'S ENQUIRY AS TO HOW HE WOULD DESCRIBE HIMSELF

● 'Like all the best families, we have our share of eccentricities, of impetuous and wayward youngsters and of family disagreements.'

THE QUEEN

● 'Deaf? If you are near there, no wonder you are deaf.'

PRINCE PHILIP, TO DEAF PEOPLE, IN REFERENCE TO A NEARBY SCHOOL'S STEEL BAND, PLAYING IN HIS HONOUR

● 'I have never drunk and never wanted to. I can never understand how anyone can get past the taste.'

PRINCESS ANNE, ON ALCOHOL

● 'I'm glad we've been bombed. It makes me feel I can look the East End in the face.'

THE QUEEN MOTHER

— ROYALS —

• 'If a cricketer, for instance, suddenly decided to go into a school and batter a lot of people to death with a cricket bat, which he could do very easily, are you going to ban cricket bats?'

> PRINCE PHILIP, RESPONDING TO CALLS TO BAN
> FIREARMS AFTER THE DUNBLANE MASSACRE

• 'Being a princess isn't all it's cracked up to be.'

> PRINCESS DIANA

• 'I now complete the process of helping my father to expose himself.'

> PRINCE CHARLES, UNVEILING A SCULPTURE
> OF PRINCE PHILIP

• 'A few years ago everybody was saying, "We must have more leisure, everybody's working too much." Now that everybody's got more leisure, they're complaining they're unemployed. They don't seem to be able to make up their minds what they want, do they?'

> PRINCE PHILIP, ON THE RECESSION

• 'Your work is the rent you pay for the room you occupy on earth.'

> THE QUEEN MOTHER

ROYALS

- 'The problem with London is the tourists. They cause the congestion. If we could just stop tourism, then we could stop the congestion.'

  PRINCE PHILIP, ON LONDON'S CONGESTION CHARGE

- 'If I'm deciding on whom I want to live with for 50 years, well, that's the last decision on which I would want my head to be ruled by my heart.'

  PRINCE CHARLES, SPEAKING IN 1972

- 'I don't think a prostitute is more moral than a wife, but they are doing the same thing.'

  PRINCE PHILIP

- 'I don't even know how to use a parking meter, let alone a phone box.'

  PRINCESS DIANA

- 'What a po-faced lot these Dutch are.'

  PRINCE PHILIP, ON A VISIT TO HOLLAND

- 'I sometimes wonder if two-thirds of the globe is covered in red carpet.'

  PRINCE CHARLES

––––––––––– **ROYALS** –––––––––––

- 'I'm doing pretty well considering. You know, in the past, when anyone left the Royal Family they had you beheaded.'

  SARAH FERGUSON

- 'I myself prefer my New Zealand eggs for breakfast.'

  THE QUEEN

- 'You can't have been here that long, you haven't got a potbelly.'

  PRINCE PHILIP, TO A BRITON RESIDING IN HUNGARY

- 'If you have a sense of duty, and I like to think I have, service means that you give yourself to people, particularly if they want you, and sometimes if they don't.'

  PRINCE CHARLES

- 'Are you Indian or Pakistani? I can never tell the difference between you chaps.'

  PRINCE PHILIP, AT A WASHINGTON EMBASSY
  RECEPTION FOR COMMONWEALTH MEMBERS

- 'I'm as thick as a plank.'

  PRINCESS DIANA

- 'I suppose, I'll now be known as Charlie's Aunt.'

  PRINCESS MARGARET

—————————— **ROYALS** ——————————

● 'Dig that crazy rhythm.'

PRINCE CHARLES, TRYING TO GET DOWN WITH
THE KIDS AT A PRINCE'S TRUST SHELTER

● 'The thing I might do best is be a long-distance
truck driver.'

PRINCESS ANNE

● 'If it has got four legs and it is not a chair, if it has two
wings and it flies but is not an aeroplane, and if it swims
and it is not a submarine, the Cantonese will eat it.'

PRINCE PHILIP, COMMENTING ON CHINESE EATING
HABITS TO A WWF CONFERENCE IN 1986

● 'I couldn't believe it the other day when I picked up a
British newspaper and read that 82% of men would
rather sleep with a goat than me.'

SARAH FERGUSON

● 'All money nowadays seems to be produced with a
natural homing instinct for the Treasury.'

PRINCE PHILIP

● 'People think that at the end of the day a man is the
only answer. Actually, a fulfilling job is better for me.'

PRINCESS DIANA

——————— ROYALS ———————

- 'I'm no angel, but I'm no Bo-Beep either.'

  PRINCESS MARGARET

- 'The Queen is most anxious to enlist everyone in checking this mad, wicked folly of "Women's Rights". It is a subject which makes the Queen so furious that she cannot contain herself.'

  QUEEN VICTORIA

- 'Aren't most of you descended from pirates?'

  PRINCE PHILIP, TO A WEALTHY RESIDENT
  OF THE CAYMAN ISLANDS

- 'Awkward, cantankerous, cynical, bloody-minded, at times intrusive, at times inaccurate and at times deeply unfair and harmful to individuals and to institutions.'

  PRINCE CHARLES, ON THE PRESS

- 'You are a pest, by the very nature of that camera in your hand.'

  PRINCESS ANNE

- 'An ugly baby is a very nasty object – and the prettiest is frightful.'

  QUEEN VICTORIA

───── ROYALS ─────

- 'Are you still throwing spears at other tribes?'

  PRINCE PHILIP, TO AN ABORIGINE ELDER,
  ON A ROYAL VISIT TO AUSTRALIA

- 'The important thing is not what they think of me, but what I think of them.'

  QUEEN VICTORIA

- 'It's like swimming in undiluted sewage'

  PRINCE CHARLES, EMERGING FROM THE SEA IN
  MELBOURNE. HIS REMARKS DIDN'T EARN HIM
  ANY BROWNIE POINTS WITH THE AUSTRALIANS,
  AND THE PRESS WENT MAD.

- 'I never see any home cooking – all I get is fancy stuff.'

  PRINCE PHILIP

- 'We've never had a holiday. A week or two at Balmoral, or ten days at Sandringham is the nearest we get.'

  PRINCESS ANNE

- 'I must confess that I am interested in leisure in the same way that a poor man is interested in money.'

  PRINCE PHILIP

- 'I'm the heir apparent to the heir presumptive.'

  PRINCESS MARGARET

— ROYALS —

● 'Ghastly.'

> PRINCE PHILIP, ON BEIJING, CHINA, IN 1986

● 'Unless one is there, it's embarrassing. Like hearing the Lord's Prayer while playing canasta.'

> THE QUEEN MOTHER, SPEAKING
> OF THE NATIONAL ANTHEM

● 'Dontopedology is the science of opening your mouth and putting your foot in it.'

> PRINCE PHILIP

● 'Everybody grows but me.'

> QUEEN VICTORIA

● 'If I hear one more joke about being hit in the face with a carnation by a Bolshevik fascist lady, I don't know what I'll do. I'm very glad it's given pleasure to everybody. It's what I'm here for.'

> PRINCE CHARLES, REFERRING TO AN INCIDENT IN
> LATVIA WHEN A 16-YEAR-OLD SCHOOLGIRL SLAPPED
> HIM IN THE FACE WITH A BUNCH OF CARNATIONS

● 'My children are not royal; they just happen to have the Queen for their aunt.'

> PRINCESS MARGARET

——— ROYALS ———

- 'How do you keep the natives off the booze long enough to get them to pass the test?'

  PRINCE PHILIP, QUIZZING A SCOTTISH
  DRIVING INSTRUCTOR

- 'Great events make me quiet and calm; it is only trifles that irritate my nerves.'

  QUEEN VICTORIA

- 'The biggest waste of water in the country is when you spend half a pint and flush two gallons.'

  PRINCE PHILIP

- 'Make a friend of your mind. Free your mind, and your bottom will follow.'

  SARAH FERGUSON, GIVING SLIMMING ADVICE

- 'It looks as if it was put in by an Indian.'

  PRINCE PHILIP, POINTING AT AN OLD-FASHIONED
  FUSE BOX WHILE ON A TOUR OF A FACTORY NEAR
  EDINBURGH IN 1993

- 'You never know, it could be somebody important.'

  QUEEN ELIZABETH II, ADVISING AN EMBARRASSED YOUNG
  WOMAN TO ANSWER HER MOBILE PHONE WHICH RANG
  WHILE THEY WERE IN CONVERSATION

ROYALS

- 'The Queen is the only person who can put on a tiara with one hand, while walking downstairs.'

  PRINCESS MARGARET

- 'I feel sure that no girl would go to the altar if she knew all.'

  QUEEN VICTORIA

- 'Who is Llewellyn?'

  PRINCE CHARLES, QUESTIONING THE NAME ON A BANNER AT HIS INVESTITURE IN WALES. LLEWELLYN WAS THE PREVIOUS PRINCE OF WALES.

- 'I rather doubt whether anyone has ever been genuinely shocked by anything I have said.'

  PRINCE PHILIP

- 'We live in what virtually amounts to a museum, which does not happen to a lot of people.'

  Prince Philip

- 'Manchester, that's not such a nice place.'

  Queen Elizabeth II

- 'You managed not to get eaten then.'

  PRINCE PHILIP, TO A STUDENT WHO HAD JUST VISITED PAPUA NEW GUINEA

——————ROYALS——————

- 'I would venture to warn against too great intimacy with artists as it is very seductive and a little dangerous.'

  QUEEN VICTORIA

QUOTATIONS ON
MARRIAGE

QUOTATIONS AND MARRIAGE

• 'Before marriage, a man will lay down his life for you; after marriage he won't even lay down his newspaper.'

HELEN ROWLAND

• 'The world has suffered more from the ravages of ill-advised marriages than from virginity.'

AMBROSE BIERCE

• 'Many a man owes his success to his first wife and his second wife to his success.'

JIM BACKUS

• 'If you want to sacrifice the admiration of many men for the criticism of one, go ahead, get married.'

KATHARINE HEPBURN

• 'Bigamy is having one wife too many. Monogamy is the same.'

OSCAR WILDE

• 'Women might be able to fake orgasms, but men can fake whole relationships.'

SHARON STONE

• 'Laugh and the world laughs with you. Snore and you sleep alone.'

ANTHONY BURGESS

QUOTATIONS AND MARRIAGE

- 'I married the first man I ever kissed. When I tell this to my children, they just about throw up.'

  BARBARA BUSH, FIRST LADY, 1989

- 'No man should marry until he has studied anatomy and dissected at least one woman.'

  HONORE DE BALZAC

- 'An archaeologist is the best husband a woman can have; the older she gets the more interested he is in her.'

  AGATHA CHRISTIE

- 'The most happy marriage I can imagine to myself would be the union of a deaf man to a blind woman.'

  S T COLERIDGE

- 'The male is a domestic animal, which, if treated with firmness, can be trained to do most things.'

  JILLY COOPER

- 'Ah Mozart! He was happily married – but his wife wasn't.'

  VICTOR BORGE

- 'If you are afraid of loneliness, don't marry.'

  CHEKHOV

——— QUOTATIONS AND MARRIAGE ———

- 'The trouble with some women is that they get all excited about nothing – and then marry him.'

  CHER

- 'One survey found that 10% of Americans thought Joan of Arc was Noah's wife…'

  ROBERT BOYNTON

- 'For a male and female to live continuously together is… biologically speaking, an extremely unnatural condition.'

  ROBERT BRIFFAULT

- 'Husbands are awkward things to deal with; even keeping them in hot water will not make them tender.'

  MARY BUCKLEY

- 'Marriage is popular because it combines the maximum of temptation with the maximum of opportunity.'

  GEORGE BERNARD SHAW

- 'The majority of husbands remind me of an orang-utan trying to play the violin.'

  JONATHAN CARROLL.

- 'If variety is the spice of life, marriage is the big can of leftover Spam.'

  JOHNNY CARSON

——— QUOTATIONS AND MARRIAGE ———

● 'Better to have loved a short man than never to have loved a tall.'

DAVID CHAMBLESS

● 'Marriage is an adventure, like going to war.'

G K CHESTERTON

● 'Marriage is like a bank account. You put it in, you take it out, you lose interest.'

IRWIN COREY

● 'I've sometimes thought of marrying, and then I've thought again.'

NOEL COWARD

● 'I feel like Zsa Zsa Gabor's sixth husband. I know what I'm supposed to do, but I don't know how to make it interesting.'

MILTON BERLE

● 'Marriage is a matter of give and take, but so far I haven't been able to find anybody who'll take what I have to give.'

CASS DALEY

QUOTATIONS AND MARRIAGE

- 'I'd marry again if I found a man who had 15 million and would sign over half of it to me before the marriage and guarantee he'd be dead within a year.'

  BETTE DAVIS

- 'Never go to bed angry. Stay up and fight.'

  PHYLLIS DILLER

- 'It destroys one's nerves to be amiable every day to the same human being.'

  BENJAMIN DISRAELI

- 'Long engagements give people the opportunity of finding out each other's character before marriage, which is never advisable.'

  OSCAR WILDE

- 'Honolulu, it's got everything. Sand for the children, sun for the wife, sharks for the wife's mother.'

  KEN DODD

- 'Any intelligent woman who reads the marriage contract, and then goes into it, deserves all the consequences.'

  ISADORA DUNCAN

——— QUOTATIONS AND MARRIAGE ———

- 'A man's wife has more power over him than the state has.'

    RALPH WALDO EMERSON

- 'Choose a wife by your ear rather than your eye.'

    THOMAS FULLER, 1732

- 'Politics doesn't make strange bedfellows, marriage does.'

    GROUCHO MARX

- 'Keep your eyes wide open before marriage, and half-shut afterwards.'

    BENJAMIN FRANKLIN

- 'Love is an ideal thing, marriage a real thing; a confusion of the real with the ideal never goes unpunished.'

    JOHANN WOLFGANG VON GOETHE

- 'Love is blind and marriage is the institution for the blind.'

    JAMES GRAHAM

- 'If I were a girl, I'd despair. The supply of good women far exceeds that of the men who deserve them.'

    ROBERT GRAVES

───── QUOTATIONS AND MARRIAGE ─────

- 'A man must marry only a very pretty woman in case he should ever want some other man to take her off his hands.'

  SACHA GUITRY

- 'Women and cats will do as they please. Men and dogs had better get used to it.'

  ROBERT HEINLEIN

- 'Sometimes I wonder if men and women really suit each other. Perhaps they should live next door and just visit now and then.'

  KATHARINE HEPBURN

- 'Bigamy is one way of avoiding the painful publicity of divorce and the expense of alimony.'

  OLIVER HERFORD

- 'Men marry because they are tired, women because they are curious; both are disappointed.'

  OSCAR WILDE

- 'Wedding is destiny, and hanging likewise.'

  JOHN HEYWOOD

QUOTATIONS AND MARRIAGE

- 'A man who marries a woman to educate her falls a victim to the same fallacy as the woman who marries a man to reform him.'

  ELBERT HUBBARD

- 'Marrying a man is like buying something you've been admiring for a long time in a shop window. You may love it when you get it home, but it doesn't always go with everything in the house.'

  JEAN KERR

- 'I don't worry about terrorism. I was married for two years.'

  SAM KINISON

- 'A coward is a hero with a wife, kids and a mortgage.'

  MARVIN KITMAN

- 'Marriage is a lottery, but you can't tear up your ticket if you lose.'

  F M KNOWLES

- 'Many a man in love with a dimple makes the mistake of marrying the whole girl.'

  STEPHEN LEACOCK

——— QUOTATIONS AND MARRIAGE ———

- 'Harpo, she's a lovely person. She deserves a good husband. Marry her before she finds one.'

  OSCAR LEVANT, TO HARPO MARX

- 'It's true that I did get the girl, but then my grandfather always said, "Even a blind chicken finds a few grains of corn now and then."'

  LYLE LOVETT, AFTER MARRYING ACTRESS JULIA ROBERTS

- 'Marriages are made in heaven and consummated on Earth.'

  JOHN LYLY

- 'Marriage is a great institution, but who wants to live in an institution?'

  GROUCHO MARX

- 'The best way to get husbands to do something is to suggest that perhaps they are too old to do it.'

  SHIRLEY MACLAINE

- 'In a novel, the hero can lay ten girls and marry a virgin for the finish. In a movie, that is not allowed. The villain can lay anybody he wants, have as much fun as he wants, cheating, stealing, getting rich and whipping servants. But you have to shoot him in the end.'

  HERMAN MANKIEWICZ

——— QUOTATIONS AND MARRIAGE ———

- 'I belong to Bridegrooms Anonymous. Whenever I feel like getting married, they send over a lady in a housecoat and hair curlers to burn my toast for me.'

  DICK MARTIN

- 'I was married by a judge. I should have asked for a jury.'

  GROUCHO MARX

- 'Eighty per cent of married men cheat in America. The rest cheat in Europe.'

  JACKIE MASON

- 'Perfection is what American women expect to find in their husbands... but English women only hope to find in their butlers.'

  W SOMERSET MAUGHAM

- 'There's a way of transferring funds that is even faster than electronic banking. It's called marriage.'

  JAMES HOLT MCGAVRAN

- 'Women want mediocre men, and men are working hard to become as mediocre as possible.'

  MARGARET MEAD

——— QUOTATIONS AND MARRIAGE ———

● 'When a man steals your wife, there is no better revenge than to let him keep her.'

SACHA GUITRY

● 'Bachelors know more about women than married men; if they didn't, they'd be married too.'

H L MENCKEN

● 'I date this girl for two years – and then the nagging starts: "I wanna know your name."'

MIKE BINDER

● 'I recently read that love is entirely a matter of chemistry. That must be why my wife treats me like toxic waste.'

DAVID BISSONETTE

● 'Marriage is like a cage; one sees the birds outside desperate to get in, and those inside desperate to get out.'

MICHEL DE MONTAIGNE

● 'Never be unfaithful to a lover, except with your wife.'

P J O'ROURKE

● 'No woman marries for money; they are all clever enough, before marrying a millionaire, to fall in love with him first.'

CESARE PAVESE

—— **QUOTATIONS AND MARRIAGE** ——

- 'It doesn't much signify whom one marries, for one is sure to find out next morning it was someone else.'

  WILL ROGERS

- 'Before marriage, a man will lie awake all night thinking about something you said; after marriage, he'll fall asleep before you finish saying it.'

  HELEN ROWLAND

- 'When you see what some girls marry, you realise how they must hate to work for a living.'

  HELEN ROWLAND

- 'Honeymoon: A short period of doting between dating and debting.'

  RAY BANDY

- 'I think men who have a pierced ear are better prepared for marriage. They've experienced pain and bought jewellery.'

  RITA RUDNER

- 'To marry is to halve your rights and double your duties.'

  ARTHUR SCHOPENHAUER

——— QUOTATIONS AND MARRIAGE ———

- 'We in the industry know that behind every successful screenwriter stands a woman. And behind her stands his wife.'

  GROUCHO MARX

- 'It is most unwise for people in love to marry.'

  GEORGE BERNARD SHAW

- 'By all means marry. If you get a good wife, you will become happy, and if you get a bad one you will become a philosopher.'

  SOCRATES

- 'Marriage: A ceremony in which rings are put on the finger of the lady and through the nose of the gentleman.'

  HERBERT SPENCER

- 'A husband is what's left of the lover after the nerve has been extracted.'

  HELEN ROWLAND

- 'I think every woman is entitled to a middle husband she can forget.'

  ADELA ROGERS ST JOHN

——— QUOTATIONS AND MARRIAGE ———

- 'Wives are people who feel they don't dance enough.'
  GROUCHO MARX

- 'Some of us are becoming the men we wanted to marry.'
  GLORIA STEINEM

- 'Someone once asked me why women don't gamble as much as men do and I gave the commonsensical reply that we don't have as much money. That was a true but incomplete answer. In fact, women's total instinct for gambling is satisfied by marriage.'
  GLORIA STEINEM

- 'Try praising your wife, even if it does frighten her at first.'
  BILLY SUNDAY

- 'Love is blind – marriage is the eye-opener.'
  PAULINE THOMASON

- 'Men have a much better time of it than women: for one thing they marry later, for another thing they die earlier.'
  H L MENCKEN

- 'Whenever I date a guy, I think, Is this the man I want my children to spend their weekends with?'
  RITA RUDNER

—— QUOTATIONS AND MARRIAGE ——

● 'God help the man who won't marry until he finds a perfect woman, and God help him still more if he finds her.'

BENJAMIN TILLETT

● 'A successful man is one who makes more money than his wife can spend. A successful woman is one who can find such a man.'

LANA TURNER

● 'Marriage isn't a word… it's a sentence.'

KING VIDOR

● 'Marriage is the one subject on which all women agree and all men disagree.'

OSCAR WILDE

● 'I guess the only way to stop divorce is to stop marriage.'

WILL ROGERS

● 'In olden times, sacrifices were made at the altar, a practice which is still very much practised.'

HELEN ROWLAND

● 'I take my wife everywhere I go. She always finds her way back.'

HENNY YOUNGMAN

—— QUOTATIONS AND MARRIAGE ——

- 'Marriage is the alliance of two people, one of whom never remembers birthdays and the other who never forgets them.'

  OGDEN NASH

- 'An ideal wife is one who remains faithful to you but tries to be just as charming as if she weren't.'

  SACHA GUITRY

- 'I should like to see any kind of a man, distinguishable from a gorilla, that some good and even pretty woman could not shape a husband out of.'

  OLIVER WENDELL HOLMES, SR.

- 'It does not matter what you do in the bedroom as long as you do not do it in the street and frighten the horses.'

  MRS PATRICK CAMPBELL

- 'A happy home is one in which each spouse grants the possibility that the other may be right, though neither believes it.'

  DON FRASER

- 'I've been asked to say a couple of words about my husband, Fang. How about "short" and "cheap"?'

  PHYLLIS DILLER

QUOTATIONS AND MARRIAGE

• 'Sexiness wears thin after a while and beauty fades, but to be married to a man who makes you laugh every day, ah, now that's a real treat.'

JOANNE WOODWARD

• 'When a girl marries, she exchanges the attentions of many men for the inattention of one.'

HELEN ROWLAND

• 'The big difference between sex for money and sex for free is sex for money costs less.'

BRENDAN FRANCIS

• 'To our wives and sweethearts… and may they never meet.'

HUGO VICKERS

• 'Marriage is like putting your hand into a bag of snakes in the hope of pulling out an eel.'

LEONARDO DA VINCI

• 'The appropriate age for marriage is around 18 for girls and 37 for men.'

ARISTOTLE

QUOTATIONS AND MARRIAGE

- 'Instead of getting married again, I'm going to find a woman that I don't like and just give her the house.'

  ROD STEWART

- 'Marriage is one of the few institutions that allow a man to do as his wife pleases.'

  MILTON BERLE

RUDE FACTS

RUDE FACTS

- On average, everyone farts once per hour.

- Farts are highly flammable.

- Adults produce between 200ml and 2l of wind per day.

- The amount you fart is increased by stress, onions, cabbage and beans.

- Vegetarians fart more, but theirs smell less.

- On average, you produce 200g of poo per day.

- Farts are created mostly by E. coli.

- A man became a tourist attraction in the Dominican Republic after admitting himself to hospital with an erection that had lasted six days.

- On average, a fart is composed of about 59% nitrogen, 21% hydrogen, 9% carbon dioxide, 7% methane and 4% oxygen. Less than 1% is what makes them stink.

- The temperature of a fart at time of creation is 98.6°F.

- Farts have been clocked at a speed of 10ft per second.

——————— RUDE FACTS ———————

- Although they won't admit it, women fart as much as men.

- Termites are the largest producers of farts.

- Bernard Clemmens of London managed to sustain a fart for an officially recorded time of 2 minutes 42 seconds.

- The word 'fart' comes from the Old English 'feortan' (meaning 'to break wind').

- The Romans made condoms from the muscle tissue of warriors they defeated in battle.

- Discovered in the foundations of Dudley Castle near Birmingham, England, were condoms that were made from fish and animal intestines and dated back to 1640.

- Casanova wore condoms made of linen.

- If you farted consistently for six years and nine months, enough gas is produced to create the energy of an atomic bomb.

- Runners sometimes drink urine to replace electrolytes

RUDE FACTS

- Dinosaur droppings are called coprolites, and are actually fairly common.

- US Navy Seals sometimes urinate in their pants during cold-water training exercises in order to stay warm.

- In Pre-Colonial Peru, the Incas washed their children's hair with urine as a remedy for head lice.

- Urinating on someone or being urinated on for enjoyment is known in fetish parlance as 'water sports'.

- Astronauts cannot burp in space. There is no gravity to separate liquid from gas in their stomachs.

- In Minnesota, the Downtown Minneapolis Neighborhood Association has initiated a campaign to prevent or eliminate public urination, which is considered a 'quality of life' criminal offence in most US cities.

- Laplanders consume a hallucinogenic mushroom called amanita muscaria, also know as Fly Agaric. The mushroom's hallucinogenic compound 'muscanol' is excreted in the urine intact. When the mushroom is in short supply, people who have consumed the mushroom will urinate into a pot. Someone without any mushrooms can then drink the urine and experience the same effects.

RUDE FACTS

- Wolves, bears, apes and other mammals use urine to claim territory, communicate eligibility for mating, body size and other individual characteristics.

- The longest recorded distance for projectile vomiting is 27ft.

- The study of nose picking is called rhinotillexomania.

- In addition to hair and blood, urine is used to test people for illicit drug use.

- In his final book *Civilization and Its Discontents*, Sigmund Freud claimed that civilisation became possible only when ancient peoples resisted the impulse to extinguish their campfires by pissing them out.

- Drinking urine is part of many non-traditional remedies used today, especially in Ayurvedic medicine.

- A party boat filled with 60 men and women capsized in Texas after all the passengers rushed to one side as the boat passed a nude beach.

- 72.4% of people place their toilet paper on the roll forward (with the loose end over the roll, towards the user).

--------------------- **RUDE FACTS** ---------------------

- The visitors at Yellowstone Park create 270 million gallons of waste per year, and use up to 18 rolls of toilet paper, per toilet, per day!

- One of the most difficult items for sewage workers to handle, as it is insoluble, yet fine enough to pass through most filtration systems, is pubic hair. Every month Thames Water removes over a ton of pubic hair at its water-treatment plants, whereupon it is taken away to a landfill site and buried.

- Ninety-eight per cent of all Americans feel better about themselves when they flush a toilet.

- Scuba divers cannot pass gas at depths of 33ft or below.

- A German who borrowed £5,000 from his mother for a penis extension demanded a refund after it ended up shorter and deformed.

- About a third of all Americans flush the toilet while they're still sitting on it.

- In the USA, more toilets flush at the half-time of the Super Bowl than at any other time of the year.

RUDE FACTS

- A Kimberly-Clark marketing survey on bathroom habits finds that, when it comes to toilet paper, women are 'wadders' and men are 'folders'.

- Twenty-two per cent of American women aged 20 gave birth while in their teens. In Switzerland and Japan, only 2% did so.

- Sex is the safest tranquilliser in the world. It is ten times more effective than valium.

- Sex gets the blood pumping and helps you sweat out booze – and it's good fun.

- Twenty-three per cent of UK employees say they have had sex in the office.

- It is estimated that The Pentagon spent $50 million on Viagra for American troops and retirees in 1999.

- For every 'normal' webpage, there are five porn pages.

- Sex is biochemically no different from eating large quantities of chocolate.

- A man's beard grows fastest when he anticipates sex.

RUDE FACTS

- The French have topped a survey as being the people who have sex the most.

- There are over 3,500 bras hanging behind the bar at Hogs and Heifers, a bar in Manhattan. So many, in fact, that they caused a beam to collapse in the ceiling.

- The average shelf-life of a latex condom is about two years.

- 'Formicophilia' is the fetish for having small insects crawl on your genitals.

- 'Ithyphallophobia' is a morbid fear of seeing, thinking about or having an erect penis.

- Internet auction site eBay has been hit by a new craze in which sellers appear naked in reflections on goods they're selling.

- The word 'gymnasium' comes from the Greek word gymnazein which means 'to exercise naked'.

- Topless saleswomen are legal in Liverpool – but only in tropical fish stores.

—————— **RUDE FACTS** ——————

- In India, it is cheaper to have sex with a prostitute than to buy a condom!

- Women who read romance novels have sex twice as often as those who don't.

- 3.9% of all women surveyed say they never wear underwear.

- An adult sex toy sparked a security scare which closed an Australian airport for nearly an hour.

- Two teenage US soldiers have been arrested for having sex in front of tourists at the Alamo.

- The Earl of Condom was a knighted personal physician to England's King Charles II in the mid-1600s. The Earl was requested to produce a method to protect the King from syphilis.

- A Cambridgeshire village has erected a 5ft-tall statue of dinosaur poo to celebrate its past.

- The world's youngest parents were eight and nine and lived in China in 1910.

RUDE FACTS

- The first couple to be shown in bed together on prime-time television were Fred and Wilma Flintstone.

- Twenty-five per cent of women think money makes a man sexier.

- Some lions mate over 50 times a day.

- Seven per cent of Americans claim they never bathe at all.

- Each day, there are over 120 million acts of sexual intercourse taking place all over the world.

- The most searched thing on yahoo.com every year is porn.

- Eight-five per cent of men who die of heart attacks during intercourse are found to have been cheating on their wives.

- Passengers at an Indian airport were shocked when a hardcore porn movie was played on television screens for 20 minutes.

- In Kentucky, 50% of the people who get married for the first time are teenagers.

RUDE FACTS

- Bird droppings are the chief export of Nauru, an island nation in the western Pacific.

- Spotted skunks do handstands before they spray.

- A couple from Germany went to a fertility clinic to find out why – after eight years of marriage – they were still childless. The cause of their trouble conceiving was that they never had sex.

- If a police officer in Coeur d'Alene, Idaho, suspects a couple is having sex inside a vehicle they must honk their horn three times, and wait two minutes before being allowed to approach the scene.

- A law in Oblong, Illinois, makes it a crime to make love while fishing or hunting on your wedding day.

- In Ames, Iowa, a husband may not take more than three gulps of beer while lying in bed with his wife.

- A law in Alexandria, Minnesota, makes it illegal for a husband to make love to his wife if his breath smells like garlic, onions or sardines.

RUDE FACTS

- A Helena, Montana law states that a woman cannot dance on a saloon table unless her clothing weighs more than 3lb 2oz.

- Hotel owners in Hastings, Nebraska, are required by law to provide a clean, white cotton nightshirt to each guest. According to the law, no couple may have sex unless they are wearing the nightshirts.

- Any couple making out inside a vehicle, and accidentally sounding the horn during their lustful act, may be taken to jail according to a Liberty Corner, New Jersey, law.

- During lunch breaks in Carlsbad, New Mexico, no couple should engage in a sexual act while parked in their vehicle, unless their car has curtains.

- In Harrisburg, Pennsylvania, it is illegal to have sex with a truck driver inside a toll booth.

- Hotels in Sioux Falls, South Dakota, are required by law to furnish their rooms with twin beds only. There should be a minimum of two feet between the beds, and it is illegal for a couple to make love on the floor between the beds.

RUDE FACTS

- In Kingsville, Texas, there is a law against two pigs having sex on the city's airport property.

- A Tremonton, Utah, law states that no woman is allowed to have sex with a man while riding in an ambulance. In addition to normal charges, the woman's name will be published in the local newspaper. The man does not receive any punishment.

- In the state of Washington, there is a law against having sex with a virgin under any circumstances (including the wedding night).

- The only acceptable sexual position in Washington DC is the missionary-style position. Any other sexual position is considered illegal.

THE BEATLES

─────────── **THE BEATLES** ───────────

- Throughout their career, the Beatles spent more than 400 weeks on the music charts.

- John Lennon was born to Julia Lennon after 30 hours of labour.

- Only 6% of the autographs in circulation from members of the Beatles are estimated to be real.

- George Harrison had a 14½ in neck.

- John Lennon was expelled from school for misbehaviour at age five.

- John and George always went to the dentist together because they were both scared.

- In the 60s, Paul had three cats named Jesus, Mary and Joseph.

- John Lennon's mother taught him how to play an Old Spanish guitar like a banjo.

- Paul used the working words 'scrambled eggs' before coming up with 'yesterday' while composing this song.

- Ringo cannot swim, except for a brief doggie paddle.

THE BEATLES

- John Lennon was raised by his mother's sister, Mimi Smith.

- Brian Epstein made the Beatles have their hair cut short after he signed them in 1962.

- By age 15, John Lennon was a big fan of Elvis.

- In 1965, John's dad Alfred made a record called 'That's My Life'.

- It has been reported that John Lennon got a big thrill out of shoplifting when he was young.

- The Beatles featured two left-handed members, Paul, whom everyone saw holding his Hoffner bass left-handed, and Ringo, whose left-handedness is at least partially to blame for his 'original' drumming style.

- John Lennon's mother died after being hit by a car.

- George was afraid of flying in an aeroplane. ✔

- Six Brazilians were turned away by immigration officials at Heathrow Airport after failing a quiz about the Beatles. The group claimed to be travelling to the UK for Liverpool's Mathew Street Festival, which celebrates the lives of the Fab Four.

—————————— **THE BEATLES** ——————————

- John used to envy his cousin Stanley's Meccano set.

- An American firm wrote to the Beatles asking if they could market the Beatles' bath water at a dollar a bottle. They refused the offer.

- 'Dear Prudence' was written by John and Paul about Mia Farrow's sister, Prudence, when she wouldn't come out and play with Mia and the Beatles at a religious retreat in India.

- Later in life, John Lennon discovered that he had dyslexia.

- Throughout their career, Ringo received far more fan mail than any of the other Beatles.

- 'Lovely Rita Meter Maid' was inspired by Paul's parking ticket from a female warden on Abbey Road in London.

- In 1962, in a contest held by a Merseyside newspaper to see who was the biggest band in Liverpool, one of the main reasons that the Beatles won was because they called in posing as different people voting for themselves.

- In 1996, Ringo Starr appeared in a Japanese advertisement for apple sauce, which coincidentally is what 'Ringo' means in Japanese.

——————— THE BEATLES ———————

- John Lennon named his band the Beatles after Buddy ✗
  Holly's 'Crickets'.

- Paul was regularly the first Beatle dressed for
  performances.

- John Lennon hated the band The Hollies.

- George Harrison didn't like the Hollies either, and had a
  specific distaste for Graham Nash.

- Without glasses, John Lennon was legally blind.

- At the end of 'A Day in the Life', an ultrasonic whistle,
  audible only to dogs, was recorded by Paul McCartney
  for his Shetland sheepdog.

- At exactly 2.58 seconds into 'Hey Jude', you can hear
  John say in the background 'I fucked it up'.

- John Lennon's favourite food was cornflakes. ✓

- Paul and Pete Best were arrested in Hamburg because
  they stuck a condom to the wall and set it on fire.

- The song 'A Day in the Life' ends with a note sustained
  for 40 seconds.

SHAKESPEARE

SHAKESPEARE

- There is no certainty that Shakespeare was born on 23 April in 1564, only that he was baptised three days later in Holy Trinity Church in Stratford-upon-Avon.

- In the Middle East, Shakespeare is referred to as Sheikh al-Subair, meaning Sheikh 'Prickly Pear' in Arabic.

- The Bard coined the phrase 'the beast with two backs' meaning intercourse in his play *Othello*.

- Shakespeare invented the word 'assassination'.

- There are only two authentic portraits of William Shakespeare.

- Anne Hathaway was 26 years old when William married her at age 18.

- All Uranus's satellites are named after Shakespearean characters.

- Shakespeare and his wife had eight children.

- The worst insult that Shakespeare used was 'you bull's pizzle'.

——————— SHAKESPEARE ———————

- Most Shakespeare plays employ verse and prose. But, while no play is composed entirely of prose, five plays are written exclusively in verse.

- At nearly 1,500 lines, Hamlet is the largest Shakespearean speaking part.

- In the 1500s, Queen Elizabeth I outlawed wife-beating after 10 p.m.

- Theatres during Elizabethan times did not have toilets, nor did the plays have intervals. Although the running times of the plays were often much shorter than they are today, audience members still felt the need to relieve themselves.

- The average American's vocabulary is around 10,000 words – Shakespeare had a vocabulary of over 29,000 words.

- William Shakespeare's will is now available to the public to read online, nearly 400 years after the great playwright put quill to paper.

- There were two Shakespeare families living in Stratford when William was born; the other family did not become famous.

--------------- SHAKESPEARE ---------------

- The Bard crudely discusses genitalia size in *The Taming of the Shrew* where the character Curtis tells Grumio, 'Away, you three-inch fool.'

- William Shakespeare dabbled in property development. At age 18, he bought the second most prestigious property in all of Stratford, The New Place, and later he doubled his investment on some land he bought near Stratford.

- Shakespeare, one of literature's greatest figures, never attended university.

- Most academics agree that William wrote his first play, *Henry VI, Part One*, around 1589 to 1590 when he would have been roughly 25 years old.

- William lived through the Black Death. The epidemic that killed over 33,000 in London alone in 1603 when Will was 39 later returned in 1608.

- Elizabethan theatres would raise a flag outside to indicate what the day's feature would be: a black flag indicated tragedy; a red, history; a white, comedy.

- The play *Cardenio* that has been credited to the Bard and which was performed in his life has been completely lost to time.

SHAKESPEARE

- Even Shakespeare had his critics. One called Robert Greene described the young playwright as an 'upstart young crow' or arrogant upstart, accusing him of borrowing ideas from his seniors in the theatre world for his own plays.

- William's 126th poem contains a farewell to 'my lovely boy', a phrase taken to imply possible homosexuality by some postmodern Shakespeare academics.

- The Bard's will gave most of his property to Susanna, his first child, and not to his wife Anne Hathaway.

- Until *The First Folio* was published seven years after his death in 1616, very little personal information was ever written about the Bard.

- Shakespeare's tombstone bears this inscription: 'Good friend, for Jesus' sake forbear to dig the dust enclosed here. Blest be the man that spares these stones, and curst be he that moves my bones'.

- The Great Bard suffered breach of copyright. In 1609, many of his sonnets were published without his permission.

---------------------- **SHAKESPEARE** ----------------------

- The famous playwright died in 1616 at the age of 52. He wrote on average 1.5 plays a year from when he first started in 1589.

- William never published any of his plays. We read his plays today only because his fellow actors John Hemminges and Henry Condell posthumously recorded his work as a dedication to their fellow actor.

- The Bard is believed to have started writing the first of his 154 sonnets in 1593 at age 29. His first sonnet was *Venus and Adonis* published in the same year.

- When reading horizontally from Shakespeare's original published copy of *Hamlet*, the furthest left-hand side reads 'I am a homosexual' in the last 14 lines of the book.

- Many expressions now taken for granted in English first appeared in Shakespeare's works, including 'elbow room', 'love letter', 'marriage bed', 'puppy dog', 'skim milk', 'wild goose chase' and 'what the dickens'.

- None of the characters in Shakespeare's plays smokes.

- Suicide occurs an unlucky 13 times in Shakespeare's plays.

SHAKESPEARE

- For centuries, English literary critics tried to disguise the fact that Shakespeare's sonnets were addressed to a male beloved.

- Some believe that *Hamlet*, written in 1599, registers Shakespeare's grief following the death of Hamnet, his boy twin, in 1596, at the age of 11.

- William was born to a Stratford tanner named John Shakespeare. His mother Mary was the daughter of a wealthy gentleman-farmer named Robert Arden.

- Legend has it that, at the tender age of 11, William watched the pageantry associated with Queen Elizabeth I's visit to Kenilworth Castle near Stratford and later recreated this scene many times in his plays.

- Unlike most famous artists of his time, the Bard did not die in poverty. When he died, his will contained several large holdings of land.

- Few people realise that, aside from writing 37 plays and composing 154 sonnets, William was also an actor who performed many of his own plays as well as those of other playwrights.

SHAKESPEARE

- As an actor performing his own plays, William performed before Queen Elizabeth I and later before James I who was an enthusiastic patron of his work.

- Of the 17,677 words that Shakespeare uses in his plays, sonnets and narrative poems, his is the first written use of over 1,700 of them.

- In the 1500s, brides carried a bouquet of flowers to hide their body odour. Hence, the custom today of carrying a bouquet when getting married.

- Bread was divided according to status. Workers got the burned bottom of the loaf, the family got the middle and guests got the top, or 'upper crust'.

- Houses had thatched roofs, with no wood underneath. It was the only place for animals to get warm. When it rained, it became slippery and sometimes the animals would slip off the roof. Hence the saying 'It's raining cats and dogs'.

- Those with money had plates made of pewter. Food with high acid content caused some of the lead to leach on to the food, causing lead poisoning death.

THE
UNDERGROUND

—————————— **THE UNDERGROUND** ——————————

- There are only two tube stations that have all five vowels in them – Mansion House and South Ealing.

- Chancery Lane has the shortest escalator on the system – 50 steps.

- The shortest distance between tube stations is Leicester Square and Covent Garden on the Piccadilly line – 0.16 miles.

- The most popular route for tourists is Leicester Square to Covent Garden on the Piccadilly line. It is quicker to walk this distance than travel on the tube.

- The only tube station that shares the name of a well-known pop group is All Saints.

- The phrase 'Mind the Gap' originated on the Northern line.

- The Jubilee line was originally going to be called the Fleet line.

- Northfields station on the Piccadilly line was the first to use kestrels and hawks to kill pigeons and stop them setting up homes in stations.

THE UNDERGROUND

- The Central line covers the longest route – from West Ruislip to Epping, you will travel 34 miles without changing.

- The Waterloo and City line covers the shortest route – 2 kilometres.

- The oldest tube line in the world is the Metropolitan line. It opened on 10 January 1863.

- Tube carriages originally had no windows and buttoned upholstery and were nicknamed 'padded cells'.

- More of the London Underground is open than in a tunnel.

- Bank has more escalators than any other station on the tube – 15, plus two moving walkways.

- Out of the 287 stations, only 29 are south of the river Thames.

- One of the female automated voice announcers is called Sonia.

- Edward Johnston designed the text font used for the London Underground in 1916.

THE UNDERGROUND

- The peak hour for tube suicides is 11am.

- People who commit suicide by throwing themselves under tube trains are called 'one-unders'. In New York, they are known as 'track pizza'.

- The Jubilee Line Extension was the most expensive railway line ever built. It cost £173 million per kilometre.

- All 409 escalators combined do the equivalent of two round-the-world trips every week.

- Amersham is not only the most westerly station on the tube but also the highest – 150 metres above sea level.

- People were smaller when the carriages were built in the 1860s – which is one of the reasons why you'll find your journey so uncomfortable today.

- Harry Beck, designer of the tube map in 1933, was only paid five guineas for his original job. His design is still the basis of today's tube map. Had he taken royalties, he would have become a very rich man.

- The first escalator was introduced at Earl's Court in 1911.

THE UNDERGROUND

- Gladstone and Dr Barnado were the only people to ever have their coffins transported by tube.

- Not only were the early escalators made of wood, but also the legs of the people who demonstrated them. Wooden-legged Bumper Harris was employed to travel up and down the tube's first escalator to prove that it was safe.

- Angel has Western Europe's longest escalator – 318 steps.

- Mosquitoes that live in the Underground have evolved into a completely different species, one that appears separated from the above-ground mozzie by over a thousand years.

- Regent's Park, Piccadilly Circus, Hyde Park Corner and Bank stations do not have an above-ground surface building.

- The air in the underground is on average 10°C hotter than the air on the surface.

- Pigeons regularly travel from West Ham in east London to central London on the tube in order to get more food.

---------------- **THE UNDERGROUND** ----------------

- Green grapes cause more accidents on the London Underground than banana skins.

- The best places to spot mice running around the tracks of the underground are Waterloo station (northbound on the Bakerloo line) and any platform at Oxford Circus.

- Anthea Turner and her sister Wendy have written a series of children's books about mice living on the London Underground.

- Only one person was ever born in a tube carriage and her name is Thelma Ursula Beatrice Eleanor. She was born in 1924 on a Bakerloo line train at Elephant & Castle, and her initials spell TUBE.

- An advertising campaign that wafted the aroma of almond liqueur through the London Underground has been dropped because the smell is similar to cyanide gas.

- Victoria and King's Cross record the highest number of tube suicides each year. This isn't surprising, as Victoria is the tube's busiest station with 85 million passengers each year and King's Cross has 70 million passengers each year.

─────────── **THE UNDERGROUND** ───────────

- Aldwych station (now closed) is featured on level 12 in the Tomb Raider game with Lara Croft killing rats.

- Christopher Lee and Donald Pleasance starred in a 1970s horror film called *Death Line* (aka *Raw Meat*), where man-eating troglodytes terrorised people on the London Underground.

- The Cadbury's Whole Nut chocolate bar is the biggest seller in the chocolate machines at tube stations.

- A fragrance called 'Madeleine' was introduced at St James's Park, Euston and Piccadilly stations in an effort to make the tube smell better on 23 March 2001. It was taken out of action on 24 March 2001, as it was making people feel sick.

- The sexiest film scene featuring the London Underground is in *The Wings of the Dove*. Helena Bonham Carter and Linus Roache travel in a 19th-century carriage together before getting off to make love in a lift.

LONDON

LONDON

- The tomb of Elizabethan poet Edmund Spenser in Westminster Abbey is said to contain unpublished works by his contemporaries, including works from William Shakespeare, who threw manuscripts into his grave to honour his genius.

- One, London is the postal address of Apsley House, the Duke of Wellington's former residence at Hyde Park Corner.

- The 'Old Lady of Threadneedle' Street is the nickname for the Bank of England, located near the Tower of London.

- St Thomas' Hospital used to have seven buildings, one for each day of the week. Supposedly, this was so staff knew on which day patients has been admitted. Only two of the buildings remain.

- Signs on Albert Bridge order troops to break step while marching over it; this is to avoid damaging the structure with the resonating vibrations.

- Before the 17ft statue of Admiral Lord Nelson was erected on top of the Trafalgar Square column in 1842, 14 stonemasons held a dinner on top of the 170ft-high pedestal.

LONDON

- The exact centre of London is marked by a plaque in the church of St Martin's-in-the-Fields overlooking Trafalgar Square, but the actual point is on the corner of Strand and Charing Cross Road, near the statue of Charles I, and there is even a plaque on the wall confirming this.

- The Monument, built to commemorate the Great Fire of London that devastated the original walled city in September 1666, is the tallest isolated stone monument in the world. It is 205ft high, and is said to be 205ft west of where the fire started in a baker's house, on Pudding Lane.

- Brixton Market was the first electrified market in the country and stands, as a result, on Electric Avenue.

- Dr Samuel Johnson once owned 17 properties in London, only one of which still survives: Dr Johnson's Memorial House in Gough Square, which contains a brick from the Great Wall of China, donated to the museum in 1822.

- The annual Notting Hill Carnival is the second largest carnival in the world after Rio de Janeiro.

LONDON

- The Monument to the Great Fire of London was intended to be used as a fixed telescope to study the motion of a single star by Robert Hooke, who designed the structure with Sir Christopher Wren.

- Postman's Park, behind Bart's hospital, is one of London's great hidden contemplative spots. It is full of memorials to 'ordinary people' who committed acts of heroism.

- The tiered design of St Bride's Church off Fleet Street is said to have inspired the traditional shape of wedding cakes.

- The nursery rhyme 'Pop Goes the Weasel' refers to the act of pawning one's suit after spending all of one's cash in the pubs of Clerkenwell.

- Oxford Street is the busiest shopping street in Europe, having over 300 shops and receiving in excess of over 200 million visitors a year, with a turnover of approximately £5 billion a year.

- The Piccadilly Circus statue known as Eros was originally intended as an angel of mercy but renamed after the Greek god of love. It was actually meant to depict the Angel of Christian Charity, and is part of a memorial to the Seventh Earl of Shaftsbury. Its stance, aiming an arrow up Shaftesbury Avenue, is thought to be a coarse visual pun.

LONDON

- The only true home shared by all four Beatles was a flat at 57 Green Street near Hyde Park, where they lived in the autumn of 1963.

- The gravestone of the famous Elizabethan actor Richard Burbage in the graveyard of St Leonard's, Shoreditch, reads simply 'Exit Burbage'.

- London was the first city to reach a population of more than a million people, in 1811. It remained the largest city in the world until it was overtaken by Tokyo in 1957.

- The Dome, the focus of the Millennium celebrations in London, is the largest structure of its kind in the world. It is big enough to house the Great Pyramid of Giza or the Statue of Liberty.

- Only six people died in the Great Fire of London, but seven people died by falling or jumping from the Monument that commemorates it before a safety rail was built.

- 'Pearly Kings and Queens', so named because of the clothes they wear, which are studded with countless pearl buttons, were originally the 'aristocracy' of the representatives of east London's traders.

LONDON

- Mayfair is named after a fair that used to be held in the area every May.

- London's smallest house is only three-and-a-half feet wide, and forms part of the Tyburn Convent in Hyde Park Place, where 20 nuns live. These nuns have taken a vow of silence and still pray for the souls of those who lost their lives on the 'Tyburn Tree', London's main execution spot until 1783, where about 50,000 people were executed. There is a plaque at the junction of Edgware Road and Marble Arch marking the site.

- Covent Garden is actually a spelling mistake! The area used to be the market garden for what is now Westminster Abbey monastery and convent.

- Inside Marble Arch is a tiny office that once used to be a police station.

- Harrods, London's most famous department store, had its beginnings in 1849 when Henry Charles Harrods opened a small grocery shop nearby on Brompton Road.

- The Houses of Parliament has 1,000 rooms, 100 staircases, 11 courtyards, eight bars, and six restaurants – none of them open to the public. The Palace of Westminster was sited by the river so it could not be totally surrounded by a mob.

LONDON

- The architect of the OXO Tower originally wanted to use electric lighting to advertise the meat-extract product, but permission was refused so he redesigned it with 'OXO' incorporated as windows on all four sides which shone out the advertising message. The building now houses restaurants, design shops and galleries.

- There is a 19th-century time capsule under the base of Cleopatra's Needle, the 68ft, 3,450-year-old obelisk on the Embankment, containing a set of British currency, a railway guide, a Bible and 12 portraits of 'the prettiest English ladies'.

- Piccadilly is named after a kind of stiff collar made by a tailor who lived in the area in the 17th century.

- The Tower of London's most celebrated residents are a colony of seven ravens. It is not known when they first settled there, but there is a legend that, should they ever desert the Tower, the kingdom and monarchy will fall.

- Only one British Prime Minister out of the 51 who have held the office since 1751, has ever been assassinated; Spencer Perceval was shot in the House of Commons in 1812.

—————————— **LONDON** ——————————

- In 1881, the Savoy Theatre became the first theatre to be lit by electricity.

- The oldest surviving bridge on the Thames Path, now the longest riverside walk, is the Clattern Bridge at Kingston, dating back to the 12th century. Richmond Bridge is the oldest surviving Thames bridge, built in 1774.

- Police are sometimes called the 'fuzz' because London police used to wear fuzzy helmets.

- Beefeaters at the Tower of London are struggling to get home contents insurance because they are judged too much of a risk. Most insurers won't give the 38 Beefeaters, who look after the Crown Jewels and live within the Tower walls, a policy.

- The inner and outer dome of St Paul's Cathedral is the second largest dome in the world, standing at 360ft high; St Peter's in Rome is the largest.

- The sculpture on top of Wellington Arch, by Adrian Jones, was added in 1912, and it is said that, before it was installed, Jones seated eight people for dinner in the body of one of the horses.

LONDON

- England's first printing press was set up in Fleet Street in the 15th century by William Caxton's assistant, remained a centre of London's publishing industry well into the late 20th century?

- The London Eye used 1,700 tonnes of steel in its construction and is heavier than 250 double-decker buses.

- Hungerford Bridge, built in 1864, is the only bridge that crosses the Thames that was built to carry both trains and pedestrians to Charing Cross.

- With a population of 7.3 million, London is the largest city in Europe. The average household size is 2.3 people.

- London contains 143 registered parks and gardens, which account for 30% of all of London's open spaces.

- There are over 300 languages spoken in the Greater London area and almost half of Britain's black and ethnic-minority residents live there, with resident communities from over 90 different countries. More than a third of Londoners belong to an ethic-minority community.

LONDON

- London is currently home to four World Heritage Sites: the Palace of Westminster, the Tower of London, Maritime Greenwich and Kew Gardens.

- Big Ben, known to most people as the four-faced clock tower of the Houses of Parliament, is actually the resonant bell on which the hours are struck. It was named after Sir Benjamin Hall, Chief Commissioner of Works when the bell was hung in 1858. Cast in Whitechapel, it was the second giant bell made for the clock, after the first became cracked during a test ringing.

WAYS TO GO

WAYS TO GO

● Every day 259200 people die.

● Clara Blandick, the actress who played Auntie Em in *The Wizard of Oz*, killed herself with sleeping pills and a plastic bag tied over her head. She was 81 years old and suffering from crippling arthritis.

● Talk-show host Ray Combs hanged himself on the night of 2 June 1996, with bed sheets in his hospital room while on a 72-hour 'suicide watch'.

● Poet Hart Crane committed suicide by drowning. While on a steamship, he bid his fellow passengers farewell and jumped overboard.

● Eighty per cent of deaths in US casinos are caused by sudden heart attacks.

● Thich Quang Duc was the Buddhist monk who famously set himself on fire on the streets of Saigon to protest against government persecution of Buddhists in 1963.

● The Pennsylvanian politician R Budd Dwyer had been convicted of bribery and conspiracy in federal court and was about to be sentenced. He called a press conference and, in front of spectators and TV cameras, he shot himself in the mouth.

----------------------WAYS TO GO----------------------

- Lillian Millicent Entwistle , actress, committed suicide in 1932 by jumping from the 'H' of the HOLLYWOOD sign.

- Joseph Goebbels, the Nazi politician, killed himself along with his wife and five children by poisoning while at Hitler's Berlin bunker in the final days of World War II.

- Thirty people a year in Canada, and 300 people a year in the US are killed by trains.

- Another Nazi politician, Hermann Goering, poisoned himself hours before he was to be executed in 1946.

- In 1998, more fast-food employees were murdered on the job than police officers.

- Singer Donny Hathaway committed suicide in 1979 by jumping from his room on the 15th floor of New York's Essex House Hotel.

- Amusement-park attendance goes up after a fatal accident. It seems many people want to ride upon the same ride that killed someone.

WAYS TO GO

- Rudolf Hess, the last surviving member of Adolf Hitler's inner circle, strangled himself in 1987 with an electrical cord aged 93 while he was the only prisoner in Spandau Prison, Berlin.

- Newscaster Chris Chubbuck shot herself in the head during a prime-time news broadcast on Florida TV station WXLT-TV in 1974. She died 14 hours later.

- Michael Hutchence, INXS band member, hanged himself with a belt in his room in the Ritz-Carlton Hotel, in Sydney, Australia.

- Writer Eugene Izzi hanged himself from an 11th-floor window on Michigan Avenue, Chicago. It was possibly an accident while he was researching a scene for a book.

- Jim Jones, the leader of a religious cult known as the People's Temple, killed himself in 1978 after watching more than 900 of his followers die from the ingestion of Kool-Ade laced with cyanide.

- Jesse William Lazear, a US physician, voluntarily infected himself with and died of yellow fever as part of Walter Reed's research in 1908.

WAYS TO GO

- More people in the United States die during the first week of the month than during the last, an increase that may be a result of the abuse of substances purchased with benefit cheques that come at the beginning of each month.

- Kiyoko Matsumoto, a 19-year-old student, died in 1933 by jumping into the 1,000ft crater of a volcano on the island of Oshima, Japan. This act started a bizarre fashion in Japan and in the ensuing months 300 children did the same thing.

- The Japanese writer Yukio Mishima committed suicide in 1979 by disembowelment and decapitation as a protest of the westernisation of Japan. He killed himself in front of an assembly of all of the students that he was teaching at a university at that time.

- Former French President Francois Maurice Marie Mitterrand died in 1996 by intentionally terminating treatment for prostate cancer.

- Roman Emperor Claudius Drusus Germanicus Nero stabbed himself with a sword in 68 AD.

- Poet Sylvia Plath committed suicide by inhaling gas from her oven.

——————————WAYS TO GO——————————

- Margaret Mary Ray, a celebrity stalker, ended her life by kneeling in front of an oncoming train in 1993.

- Socrates was required to drink hemlock to end his life after being found guilty of corrupting the youth of Athens.

- Van Gogh shot himself in 1890 and died two days later.

- Horace Wells, who pioneered the use of anaesthesia in the 1840s, was arrested for spraying two women with sulphuric acid; he anaesthetised himself with chloroform and slashed open his thigh with a razor in 1848.

- Japanese and Chinese people die on the fourth of the month more often than any other dates. The reason may be that they are 'scared to death' by the number four. The words four and death sound alike in both Chinese and Japanese.

- People with initials that spell out GOD or ACE are likely to live longer than people whose initials spell out words like APE, PIG, or RAT.

- Virginia Woolf committed suicide by drowning in 1941.

———————— WAYS TO GO ————————

- In 1978, actor Gig Young shot and killed his wife of three weeks, Kim Schmidt, then shot himself.

- Writer Sherwood Anderson, swallowed a toothpick at a cocktail party. He died of peritonitis on an ocean liner bound for Brazil.

- John Jacob Astor drowned with the 'unsinkable' *Titanic*.

- Attila the Hun bled to death from a nosebleed on his wedding night.

- Alexander I of Greece died from blood poisoning after being bitten by his gardener's pet monkey.

- Alexander II, Czar of Russia 1855–81, was assassinated by a bomb which tore off his legs, ripped open his belly and mutilated his face.

- Jane Austen died of Addison's disease in 1871.

- Sir Francis Bacon died of pneumonia. He was experimenting with freezing a chicken by stuffing it with snow.

- Velma Barfield was the first woman executed in the US since the restoration of the death penalty in 1967.

WAYS TO GO

- Thomas a Becket, Archbishop of Canterbury, was murdered in the Canterbury cathedral in 1170 by four knights, supposedly on the orders by Henry II.

- Ludwig van Beethoven died in 1827 of cirrhosis of the liver.

- Actor John Belushi died of a drug overdose in 1982.

- Rainey Bethea was the last publicly executed criminal in the US, and was hanged in 1936.

- Bridget Bishop was the first of the supposed witches hung in Salem, Massachusetts. She was executed on 10 June 1692.

- Salvatore 'Sonny' Bono crashed into a tree while skiing in 1998.

- Charles Brooks, Jr. was the first criminal to be executed in the US by lethal injection.

- Calamity Jane died in 1903 from pneumonia following a bout of heavy drinking.

- Al Capone died of syphilis in 1947.

--------------------WAYS TO GO-------------------

- Singer Karen Carpenter passed away from heart failure caused by anorexia nervosa, at age 32.

- Actor Jack Cassidy died in a fire, while asleep on the couch in his apartment.

- Catherine the Great, Empress of Russia, had a stroke, while going to the bathroom.

- Romanian President Nicolae Ceausescu was executed in 1989 by firing squad, on live television, along with his wife.

- Diver Sergei Chalibashvili attempted a three-and-a-half reverse somersault in the tuck position during the World University Games. On the way down, he smashed his head on the board and was knocked unconscious. He died after being in a coma for a week.

- Cleveland Indians baseball player Raymond Johnson Chapman died in 1920 after being struck on the head by a baseball pitch, becoming the only player ever killed as a result of a major-league baseball game.

- Conor Clapton, son of musician Eric Clapton, fell out of a 53rd-floor window at the age of five.

--------- WAYS TO GO ---------

- Cleopatra committed suicide by poison, supposedly from an asp, a venomous snake, in 30 BC.

- Nat 'King' Cole died of complications following surgery for lung cancer.

- Explorer Christopher Columbus died in 1506 from rheumatic heart disease.

- Actor Bob Crane was murdered in his hotel room in 1976.

- Singer Jim Croce was the victim of a plane crash in 1973. The plane crashed into a tree 200 yards past the end of the runway while taking off from Natchitoches, Louisiana, Municipal Airport.

- Marie Curie, the chemist who discovered Radium, died of leukaemia, caused by exposure to radiation.

- Mass murderer Jeffrey Dahmer was beaten to death with a broomstick by a fellow inmate at the Columbia Correctional Institute.

- Albert Dekker, actor and California legislator, was suffocated by hanging from a shower curtain rod while being handcuffed and wearing women's lingerie.

WAYS TO GO

- According to a British law passed in 1845, attempting to commit suicide was a capital offence. Offenders could be hanged for trying.

- Edward Despard was the last executed criminal to be drawn and quartered in England in 1803.

- Trombonist Tommy Dorsey choked to death in his sleep, because of food that had lodged in his windpipe.

- Philanthropist Anthony J Drexel III shot himself accidentally while showing off a new gun in his collection to his friends.

- Jessica Dubroff died at the age of seven in 1996 in a plane crash, while attempting to become the youngest pilot to fly cross-country.

- Actress Isadora Duncan was killed through accidental strangulation when her scarf caught in car wheel.

- Nelson Eddy suffered a stroke while entertaining on stage in Miami Beach. He died the next day.

- Colombian soccer player Andres Escobar was murdered by unknown thugs, apparently in anger over the accidental goal he had scored for the US during a World Cup game.

———————WAYS TO GO———————

- Horror-filmmaker Michael Findlay was decapitated by helicopter blade in 1977.

- Jim Fixx, who made jogging popular, died of a heart attack while jogging.

- Actor Eric Fleming drowned when his canoe capsized during the filming of a movie near the headwaters of the Amazon in the Haullaga River, Peru.

- Rajiv Gandhi, prime minister of India from 1984 until 1989, was killed by a bomb hidden in a bouquet of flowers, which exploded in his hand.

- Judy Garland took an overdose of sleeping pills in 1969.

- Marvin Gaye was murdered on his birthday in 1984 by his father.

- Musician John Glasscock died of a heart infection caused by an abscessed tooth.

- Russian figure skater Sergei Grinkov died of a heart attack during skating practice.

- Henry Gunther was the last soldier killed in WWI.

————————WAYS TO GO————————

- Alexander Hamilton, former US Treasury Secretary, was shot in 1804 by US Vice President Aaron Burr in a pistol duel near Weehawken, New Jersey.

- World War I spy Mata Hari was executed by firing squad; she refused a blindfold and threw a kiss to the executioners.

- Leslie Harvey, lead guitarist of the Glasgow band Stone the Crows, died after being electrocuted on stage at Swansea's Top Rank Ballroom on 3 May 1972.

- WWF wrestler Owen Hart died while performing a stunt in the wrestling ring. He was being lowered into the ring by a cable, when he fell 70ft to his death, snapping his neck.

- Actress Elizabeth Hartman fell to her death from a fifth-floor window in a bizarre echo of a character in her 1966 movie *The Group*.

- Jockey Frank Hayes died from a heart attack during a race. His horse, Sweet Kiss, won the race, making Hayes the only deceased jockey to win a race.

- Ernest Miller Hemingway committed suicide with a shotgun.

WAYS TO GO

- Margaux Hemingway committed suicide in 1996 with an overdose of a sedative. She was the fifth person in her family to take their own life.

- Actor Jon-Erik Hexum playfully shot himself with a blank-loaded pistol on the set of TV spy show *Cover Up*. The concussion forced a chunk of his skull into his brain; he died six days later.

- Actor William Holden was found dead in his apartment. He had been drinking, and apparently fell, struck his head on an end table and bled to death.

- John C Holmes, porn film star, died through complications of AIDS in 1988.

- Harry Houdini died of a ruptured appendix. He died on Halloween.

- Actor Leslie Howard (Ashley Wilkes in *Gone With the Wind*) was killed when his civilian plane was shot down by German fighter planes during WWII.

- Rock Hudson died of AIDS. He was the first major public figure to announce he had AIDS.

————————WAYS TO GO ————————

- William Huskisson was the first person killed by a train. His death occurred in 1830 when he was attending the opening of the Liverpool–Manchester Railway. As he stepped on the track to meet the Duke of Wellington, Stephenson's 'Rocket' hit him. He died later that day.

- Hal Mark Irish was killed in a leap from a hot-air balloon in what was believed to be the first US death from the thrill sport of bungee jumping. Irish fell more than 60ft to his death on 29 October 1991, after breaking loose from his bungee cord during a demonstration.

- German spy Josef Jakobs was the last person to be executed in the Tower of London in 1941.

- Thomas Jefferson died of dysentery in 1826. He died on the 50th anniversary of the signing of The Declaration of Independence, and the same day as John Adams.

- Olympic cyclist Knut Jensen died of a fractured skull during the 1960 Olympics in Rome. In the 93° heat, he collapsed from sunstroke and hit his head. He was one of only two athletes to die as a result of Olympic competition.

- Brian Jones, musician and one-time Rolling Stone, drowned in his swimming pool while drunk and on drugs.

——————WAYS TO GO——————

- Spanish bullfighter Joselito was fatally gored fighting his last bull in 1920.

- Vladimir Komarov was the first cosmonaut to die in space.

- Mary Jo Kopechne drowned when the car she was a passenger in, driven by Senator Edward Kennedy, plunged off a bridge in 1969.

- Olympic runner Francisco Lazaro collapsed towards the end of the 1912 Olympic marathon in Stockholm.

- Brandon Lee was shot by a gun firing blanks, while filming the movie *The Crow*. His missing scenes were later filled in by computer animation.

- Bruce Lee died suddenly in 1973 from a swollen brain.

- Actress Jayne Mansfield died in a car accident in 1967. Her wig flew off in the impact, leading to rumours that she had been decapitated.

- Mark Maples was the first person to be killed on a ride in Disneyland. He stood up while riding the Matterhorn Bobsleds and was thrown to his death.

--------------------- WAYS TO GO ---------------------

- Bill Masterton, hockey player for Minnesota North Stars, fell over backwards and hit his head on the ice after being checked during a game against the Oakland Seals. His is the only death in pro-hockey during the modern era.

- Kenneth Allen McDuff is thought to be the only person ever freed from death row and then returned after killing again. He was executed by injection on 17 November 1998, in Huntsville, Texas.

- William McKinley, 25th US President, died of gangrene. He was shot by an assassin and his wounds were not properly dressed.

- Margaret Mitchell, author of *Gone With the Wind*, was crossing an Atlanta street on her way to the theatre when she was hit by a speeding cab. She died of her injuries five days later.

- Actor Vic Morrow died in a helicopter accident on the set of *Twilight Zone – The Movie*.

- Laura Patterson, professional bungee jumper, was killed during rehearsals for the Super Bowl at the New Orleans Superdome. She died of massive head injuries.

WAYS TO GO

- French highwayman Nicolas Jacques Pelletier was the first person beheaded with the guillotine.

- Pope Johann XII was beaten to death in 963, at age 18, by the husband of a woman with whom he was having an affair.

- Grigory Rasputin was assassinated in 1916. He had been poisoned (cyanide), shot (three times) and thrown into a river.

- Keith Relf, musician in The Yardbirds, was electrocuted while playing guitar in the bathtub.

- John Augustus Roebling, designer of the Brooklyn Bridge, died of a tetanus infection after having his leg crushed by a ferryboat while working on the Brooklyn Bridge.

- Julius and Ethel Rosenberg were executed in the electric chair on 19 June 1953. They were the first husband-and-wife team executed in the US. They had been charged with espionage and spying.

- Singer Selena was shot by the president of her fan club in 1995.

—————— WAYS TO GO ——————

- Fencer Vladimir Smirnov died of brain damage. During a fencing match against Matthias Behr, Behr's foil snapped, pierced Smirnov's mask, penetrated his eyeball and entered his brain. Smirnov died nine days later.

- Actor Yoshiuki Takada died in 1985. The Sankai Juku Dance Company of Toyko had been performing *The Dance Of Birth And Death* on the side of Seattle's Mutual Life building when Takada's rope broke and he plunged six storeys to his death.

- Musician Tommy Tucker died of carbon tetrachloride poisoning sustained while he was finishing floors in his home.

- Sir William Wallace, Scottish rebel, was executed in 1305 by being hanged for a short time, taken down still breathing and having his bowels torn out and burned. His head was then struck off, and his body divided into quarters, in the punishment known as 'hanged, drawn and quartered'.

- Playwright Tennessee Williams choked to death on a nose-spray bottle cap that accidentally dropped into his mouth while he was using the spray.

MISCELLANEOUS

MISCELLANEOUS

- Because of our modern diet of food preservatives, undertakers have been noticing that dead people do not deteriorate as fast as they once did.

- More babies are born in September than in any other month. ✗

- The world's heaviest man, Robert Earl Hughes, died in 1958 aged 32. He weighed 86 stone 3 pounds. His chest measured 124in.

- A melcryptovestimentaphiliac is someone who compulsively steals ladies underwear.

- If a man shaves with a razor, he uses more energy than if he uses an electric shaver because of the power required to purify and pump the water through his tap. ✓

- Jim Bristoe, an American, invented a 30ft-long, 2-ton pumpkin cannon that can fire pumpkins up to five miles.

- Over the past 25 years, 5,000 million Smarties lids have been produced. Some rare lids are collectors' items.

- There are more people over 60 than there are under 16. By 2015, almost a quarter of the population will be over 60. ✗

MISCELLANEOUS

- Every weekday morning, the commuters of Los Angeles use 250,000 gallons of gas getting to work. They drive five million miles, which would be like one car driving to the moon and back 20 times, or around the earth 192 times.

- Alfred the Great founded 25 towns, established schools and published a collection of laws.

- A dinomaniac is someone with the compulsive urge to dance.

- Henry I nominated his daughter, Matilda, as successor. On his death, the throne was offered to his nephew, as a woman was considered unfit to rule.

- An ergasiophobe is someone who is afraid of work.

- There are more coffee drug addicts in the US than drug addicts of any other kind.

- Adolf Hitler was a vegetarian.

- In mid-2001, an estimated 8,100 Britons were aged 100 and over. By 2015, there will be three times as many men and twice as many women over 100 as there are now.

—————— MISCELLANEOUS ——————

- Kathryn Ratcliffe set a world record by eating 138 Smarties in three minutes using chopsticks at the Metro Centre, Gateshead in 2003.

- American Indians used the spurs on the legs of male turkeys as projectiles on arrowheads.

- Marijuana is Spanish for 'Mary Jane'.

- The words 'flammable' and 'inflammable' mean the same. 'Inflammable' is grammatically correct, but it was feared that safety hazards would result when people mistook 'inflammable' to mean 'not capable of producing flames'.

- A rouleau is another name for coins wrapped in a roll of paper.

- In Ventura County, California, cats and dogs are not allowed to have sex without a permit.

- Car number plates ending in four have been banned in Beijing because they are said to be unlucky.

- Old-fashioned Chinese typewriters have 5,700 characters.

- There are more plastic flamingoes in the United States than real ones.

———————— MISCELLANEOUS ————————

- For every ton of fish that is caught in all the oceans on our planet, there are three tons of rubbish dumped into the oceans.

- In many states (in the USA) the highway patrol carries two gallons of Coke in the trunk to remove blood from the highway after a car accident.

- A misomaniac is someone who hates everything.

- Newborn babies are given to the wrong mother in the hospital 12 times a day worldwide.

- On 17 February 1930, the first flight by a cow in an airplane was recorded. The milk produced by the cow during the flight was put into containers and parachuted over the city of St Louis.

- The tradition of pumpkin carving is Irish. It started with the carving of turnips but, when the Irish immigrated to the US, they found pumpkins were easier to carve.

- A traditional Christmas dinner in early England was the head of a pig prepared with mustard.

——————— MISCELLANEOUS ———————

- Superstition says, if you cry on Chinese New Year's Day, you will cry all through the year so children are tolerated and not disciplined.

- For the first time in history, the number of people on the planet aged 60 or over will soon surpass those under five.

- An erythrophobe is someone who blushes easily.

- In Ancient Poland, it was believed that sprinkling sugar on the bride's bouquet kept her temper sweet. ✓

- In the past, Christmas trees were only kept indoors for one night.

- The average baby spends 27.5 months in nappies.

- The WD in WD-40 stands for water displacer.

- More people are born on 5 October in the United States than any other day.

- The world record for balancing people on your head is 92 in one hour.

—————— MISCELLANEOUS ——————

- The wedding bouquet for Ancient Greeks and Romans, was a pungent mix of garlic and herbs or grains (garlic to ward off evil spirits and herbs to ensure a fruitful union).

- In Chinese tradition, knives or scissors should not be used on New Year's Day as this may cut off fortune.

- Seventy-five per cent of people wash from top to bottom in the shower.

- In California, you are not permitted to wear cowboy boots unless you already own at least two cows.

- The fear of Halloween is called samhainophobia.

- Methyphobia is fear of alcohol.

- Parts of the dead sea scrolls appeared for sale in the 1 June 1954 issue of the *Wall Street Journal*.

- Today, an astonishing 570,000 tubes of Smarties are made every day, with an estimated 16,000 Smarties eaten per minute in the UK. There are an average of 48 Smarties in every tube.

- The Chinese symbol which looks like two women standing in one house means 'trouble'.

---------------------- **MISCELLANEOUS** ----------------------

- The most common recipient of Valentine cards are school teachers.

- Strange college courses include advanced cereal science, ✓ amusement park administration, clay wheel throwing, fatherhood and soil judging.

- Genitofemoral neuropathy means 'Jeans are too tight'.

- US students read an average of 60,000 pages in four years.

- A 1969 Iowa state college study showed that a parent's stress level at the time of conception is a major factor in determining the child's sex. The child is usually the same sex as the less stressed parent.

- A misodoctakleidist is someone who hates practising the piano.

- Twenty-seven per cent of Americans think billboards are beautiful.

- An arithmomaniac is someone who counts things compulsively.

- In Bhutan, all citizens officially become a year older on ✓ New Year's Day.

MISCELLANEOUS

- Someone on Earth reports seeing a UFO every three minutes. In the US, reported sightings are most likely to occur in July, at 9 p.m. or 3 a.m.

- 'Wassail' comes from the Norse 'ves heill', to be of good health. Wassail is the tradition of visiting neighbours on Christmas Eve and drinking to their health.

- A suriphobe is someone who is afraid of mice.

- In the US, 26 August is National Cherry Popsicle Day.

- In California, the owners of houses with Christmas lights on them past 2 February may be fined up to $250.

- Jack-o'-lantern derives its name from British folktale character – the soul of someone barred from both heaven and hell and condemned to wander the earth with his lantern.

- It is estimated that 93% of American children will go out trick or treating for Halloween.

- In the past 40 years, the number of over-65s in Britain has doubled.

- An erythrophobe is someone who blushes easily.

MISCELLANEOUS

- Ninety-nine per cent of pumpkins sold in the US are for the sole purpose of decoration.

- Ukrainians prepare a traditional 12-course Christmas meal. The youngest child watches through the window for the evening star to appear, a signal that the feast can begin.

- In the US, 15 August is National Relaxation Day.

- A dinomaniac is someone with the compulsive urge to dance.

- For over 6,000 years, aboriginal people killed buffalo by driving them to jump sites. The town of 'Head-smashed-in-Buffalo-Jump' in Alberta, Canada, has among the largest of these jump sites.

- All racehorses in the US celebrate their birthday on 1 January.

- London Eye passengers reach 135 metres above the London skyline – 30 metres higher than the previous tallest observation wheel in Yokohama Bay.

- Canada declared national beauty contests cancelled as of 1992, claiming they were degrading to women.

MISCELLANEOUS

- People do not get sick from cold weather; it's from being indoors a lot more.

- 'Adcomsubordcomphibspac' is the longest acronym. It is a Navy term standing for Administrative Command, Amphibious Forces, Pacific Fleet Subordinate Command.

- One in twelve Americans alphabetises their spice rack.

- An American house cat eats more beef per year than an average person in Central America.

- The Ancient Greeks called our galaxy the Milky Way because they thought it was made from drops of milk from the breasts of the Greek goddess Hera.

- Yuri Gagarin survived the first manned space flight but was killed in a plane crash seven years later.

- An algologist studies seaweed.

- Astronauts' footprints and Lunar Rover tyre tracks will stay on the moon for millions of years, as there is no wind to blow them away.

MISCELLANEOUS

- An artificial spider and web are often included in the decorations on Ukrainian Christmas trees. A spider web found on Christmas morning is believed to bring good luck.

- If the government passed a law that all the outdoor lighting in the US had to be provided by low-pressure sodium light bulbs, then they would save enough money to pay for every college student's tuition.

- The world's largest palace has 1,788 rooms. It was built for the Sultan of Brunei.

- The world's largest recorded gathering of people was at a Hindu religious festival in India in 1989. It was attended by about 15 million people.

- Abraham Lincoln went to school for less than a year. He taught himself to read and write.

- An anemophobic is someone afraid of high winds.

- The longest recorded swim was 2,938 km down the Mississippi River in 1930. The swimmer spend 742 hours in the water.

MISCELLANEOUS

- The longest jail sentence passed was in the United States – 10,000 years for a triple murder.

- Levi Strauss made the first pair of blue jeans in 1850. They were intended as work trousers for American miners looking for gold.

- In Ancient Rome, only important people wore purple clothes. This is because the purple dye came from a particular kind of shellfish and was very expensive.

- The Christmas tree tradition was started in 16th century Germany by Martin Luther, a German theologian.

- If you could count the number of times a cricket chirps in one minute, divide by 2, add 9 and divide by 2 again, you would have the correct temperature in degrees Celsius.

- If you had 15 cubes numbered 1 to 15 and you tried to line them up in every possible sequence, and if you made a change every minute, it would take you 2,487,996 years to do it.

- If you stroke a cat 70 million times, you will have developed enough static electricity to light a 60-watt light bulb for one minute.

————————— **MISCELLANEOUS** —————————

- If you travelled at the speed of light, it would only take you 0.0000294 seconds to climb Mt. Everest.

- Being unmarried can shorten a man's life by ten years.

- 111,111,111 x 111,111,111 = 12,345,678,987,654,321.

- Adults have, on average, 2 gallons of air in the space between their skin and their clothes.

- A forgetful grandfather won £200,000 in Australia after he accidentally bought three tickets for the same lottery draw.

- A Googol is the mathematical term for a 1 followed by 100 zeros.

- World War II veterans are now dying at the rate of about 1,100 each day.

- In 2002, the most popular boat name in the US was *Liberty*.

- The Amazon rainforest produces half the world's oxygen supply. ✓

─────────────── **MISCELLANEOUS** ───────────────

• If you were to go on holiday for eleven days, you'd have less than one million seconds to enjoy it.

• Beaver Lake, in Yellowstone Park, USA, was artificially created by beaver damming.

• Off the coast of Florida, there is an underwater hotel. Guests have to dive to the entrance. ✓

• Over 4 million cars in Brazil are now running on gasohol instead of petrol. Gasohol is a fuel made from sugar cane.

• In the USA, firearms and tobacco are the only consumer products available on the market not subject to any federal health and safety standards. ✓

• The longest throw of a fresh egg – without breaking it – is 98.51 metres. The record was achieved in Texas in 1978.

• The world record for pancake flipping is 349 flips in two minutes and the largest pancake ever tossed measured 15m in diameter.

• An average ballpoint pen can write a line 2 miles long. ✓

———————— **MISCELLANEOUS** ————————

- The significance of the number 21 in a 21-gun salute is derived from adding the digits of 1776.

- The Empire State Building has 6,400 windows.

- It is considered an insult to tip at a restaurant in Iceland. ✓

- Names for Atlantic hurricanes can be only French, English or Spanish.

- Twelve per cent of lightning strikes occur at golf courses.

- A light bulb at a fire station in Livermore, California, has been burning since 1901.

- Queen Isabella of Spain was the first woman to be featured on a U.S. postage stamp.

- Times Square was originally called Long Acre Square.

- The 'F' word is used 246 times in the movie *Goodfellas*.

- Fifty-seven per cent of women would rather go on a shopping spree than have sex.

- Sixty-three per cent of pet owners sleep with their pets.

MISCELLANEOUS

- The average American receives their first romantic kiss at age 13.

- There are twice as many billionaires in the US today as there were ten years ago.

- More than half-a-million trees are used every Sunday to produce America's Sunday newspapers.

- Forty-eight per cent of men think balding has a negative effect on business and social relationships.

- In 1948, 2.3% of American households had televisions. Today 99% do.

- The name Jeep came from the abbreviation used in the army for the 'General Purpose' vehicle, 'GP'.

- One million Americans wear false teeth. Approximately half of these are radioactive. There is a tiny amount of uranium in these teeth to make them whiter in incandescent light.

- In 1998, 58% of American adults were married and living with their spouses, an all-time low.

MISCELLANEOUS

- The top three products for coupon redemption are cold cereal, soap and deodorant.

- Once every month, *National Geographic* publishes a stack of magazines 52 miles tall.

- A special matchmaking agency has been set up in China to serve people who want sexless marriages.

- Forty-six per cent of violence on TV occurs in cartoons.

- Only about 5% of people dream in colour.

- Eighty-five per cent of parents use child safety seats incorrectly.

- The ratio of people to TVs in the world is six to one.

- The average American male laughs 69 times a day where the average woman laughs 55 times a day.

- Males make 85% of all obscene calls.

- Life expectancy for Russian men has actually gone down over the past 40 years. A Russian male born today can expect to live an average 58 years.

—————————— MISCELLANEOUS ——————————

● Five per cent of Americans never get married.

● If a girl owns one Barbie, she most likely owns seven.

● Fifty per cent of American adults attended an arts activity in 1997.

● People aged 24–35 worry less than adults of other age groups.

● Five per cent of Americans say they 'never' make their beds.

● The average person moves their residence 11 times in their life, about once every six years.

● Thirty-five per cent of people watching TV yell at it.

● One in seven Americans can't locate the US on a map.

● Only 30% of US adults actually have dandruff while 50% are 'self conscious about it'.

● Thirty-two per cent of women and 8% of men say they are better at doing laundry than their spouse.

● In 1985, the most popular waist size for men's trousers was 32. By 2003, it was 36.

MISCELLANEOUS

- A Brussels Airlines flight to Vienna was aborted because the pilot was attacked in the cockpit. The attacker was a passenger's cat, who got out of its travel bag.

- Thirteen per cent of the letters in a given book are 'e'.

- The average age kids begin to use a microwave is seven.

- The average American uses 730 crayons by the age of ten.

- Sixty-three per cent of American adults will rent at least one video this month.

- The average sleeper rolls over 12 times in bed per night.

- The Pentagon uses an average of 666 rolls of toilet paper each day.

- More babies are conceived in December than any other month.

- About 8% of the students at the Dunkin Doughnuts training centre fail the six-week course.

- The average speed of a golf ball in flight during the PGA tour is 160mph.

——————— MISCELLANEOUS ———————

- Eight-five per cent of phone calls are conducted in the English language.

- Ninety-nine per cent of India's truck drivers can't read ✓ road signs.

- There are now 47,355 female millionaires aged between 18 and 44 in Britain.

- You can now buy a coffin which can be used as a wine rack, table, and/or bookcase before you are buried in it.

- Three per cent of all photos taken in the US are taken at Disney Land or Disney World.

- Nearly 6% of all marriage proposals are made over the telephone.

- Each year, more people are killed by teddy bears than by grizzly bears. ✓

- A chef's hat is shaped the way it is to allow air to circulate around the scalp, keeping the head cool in a hot kitchen.

- Sixty per cent of American babies are named after relatives.

―――――――――― **MISCELLANEOUS** ――――――――――

- Over 15 billion prizes have been given away in cracker jack boxes.

- $26 billion has been paid out in ransom in the United States in the last 20 years.